AN OPINIONATED GUIDE

Erotic Art

HOXTON MINI PRESS

Why care about erotic art?

Sex is everywhere – woven into flimsy bestsellers bought in airport lounges, studied in great works of literature, film and music and splayed upon billboards worldwide. Even in the most mundane places, sex lingers, promising thrill, catharsis and escape. Yet its depiction remains taboo.

In 2021, Transport for London rejected advertisements from the Vienna Tourist Board featuring Egon Schiele's nude figures, deeming them too 'shocking'. In Moscow, an erotic art museum was attacked by Orthodox Christians, who stormed the building carrying bricks and Bibles. Even in the digital age, artists face censorship on social media platforms, with painter Betty Tompkins' account suspended after posting a photograph of her exhibition catalogue.

Today, much erotic art is still regarded as too scandalous and transgressive, often relegated to dusty back shelves by feelings of embarrassment and shame. What is even considered erotic also varies from person to person, making erotic art elusive and complicating the line between art and pornography. And yet, as psychiatrist Anthony Storr writes: 'Sex is so important, so pervasive... it cannot be separated from the person as a whole.' Erotic art has (throughout history) empowered people to embrace and liberate this essential part of themselves.

Ultimately, erotic art does not aim to resolve these complexities; instead, it reflects human nature in all its contradictions, holding a mirror to the world and its diverse desires.

The short

story of

erotic art

Erotic art is about far more than just sex – it tells us stories of civilisation itself, reflecting love, politics, religion and revolution. It chronicles a tumultuous past across painting, sculpture, film and photography, with fragments of erotic lives persisting even in societies where sexual imagery was condemned. Unearthed by archaeologists and art historians, forgotten works reveal the intimate histories of long-lost civilisations – and the complexities of human desire. From the joyful artistic expressions of the sexual shenanigans of Greco-Roman gods to the erotic sculptures at India's Khajuraho temples celebrating the divine connection between sexuality and spirituality, the history of erotic art is intertwined with profound questions relating to our existence and identity.

Venus figurines *25,000 BCE*

Offering a glimpse into lost societies, figures like the *Venus of Willendorf* (p.18) embody a mysterious, primitive eroticism. More than 200 Venus figurines have been found, and are recognised as some of the earliest forms of prehistoric artwork.

Ancient Egypt *3100 BCE–30 BCE*

An enduring need for sex and intimacy also reveals itself through Ancient Egyptian artefacts like the 1150 BCE *Turin Erotic Papyrus*, containing often humorous scenes and considered by many to be the first erotic artwork, showing desires that remain familiar to us today.

Seduction in Greek & Roman Art *800 BCE–476 CE*

In Ancient Greece and Rome, erotic art was just as concerned with mortal pleasure as with the exploits of the divine. Many of Pompeii's frescoes (p.24) depict women receiving pleasure as much as men, with cunnilingus, fellatio, threesomes and orgies all memorialised onto its walls. Pottery from this era features vibrant scenes of intimacy, fornicating figures in hues of ochre or ink-black, fucking, sucking or simply tenderly embracing.

Love and celebration in Indian Art and the Kamasutra *400 BCE*

Reconnecting the erotic and the sacred, sex is celebrated in Indian art as a guiding principle for leading a rich spiritual life. The reliefs of dance, song and intercourse in the towering temples of Khajuraho (p.26) show procreation and the abundance represented by the human body as a route to the divine in Hinduism and Jainism. Manuscripts like the *Kamasutra* inspired detailed illustrations of lovers, highlighting sensuality as vital for emotional fulfilment.

Veiled medieval passions & manuscripts *500–1500*

The Middle Ages saw a rise in Christian iconography filled with expressions of sensuality. Various spiritual mystics gained notoriety, their writings describing erotic visions of Christ veiled in the language of rapture. Suggestive renderings of Christ's side wound further blended Christian spirituality with sensuality, as seen in the ornate, Catholic illuminated manuscript *Prayer Book of Bonne de Luxembourg* (p.30).

Eroticism & idealism in the Renaissance *1300s–1650*

Marking a revival of antiquity, the Renaissance brought the focus back to realism and the beauty of the human body, placing humans, rather than the divine, at the centre of discourse. Titian's *Venus of Urbino* (p.34) epitomises this union of eroticism and idealism. Artists in Florence celebrated both sacred and sensual themes, reflecting a shift towards embracing eroticism as an integral part of art and culture during this transformative period.

Japan's erotic art and the Golden Age of Shunga *1603–1868*

Japan boasts a rich history of erotic art, particularly through Shunga, the widely appreciated explicit imagery that was typically created as woodblock print or hand-painted scrolls. Reverberating through the 20th and 21st centuries, artists like Nobuyoshi Araki and Daidō Moriyama (p.110) sought to modernise the art form, producing striking, graphic photographic works that pay homage to this erotic heritage.

Decadent desires at court, from Baroque to Rococo *1700s*

Erotic art flourished in the French court where the Baroque style emerged, celebrating pleasure and grandeur. Countering Protestantism's po-faced simplicity, Baroque revelled in detail, movement and grandeur. Giving way to Rococo, a lighter, more whimsical style, artists like Fragonard (p.42) tapped into the mood by depicting sexual fantasies and newfound freedoms, intertwining flirtation with a playful escapism.

The Marquis de Sade & sadomasochism *1780s*

During the chaos of the French Revolution, the opulence of the once-dominant Baroque and Rococo styles was dismantled. In this tumultuous environment, infamous libertine the Marquis de Sade wrote *120 Days of Sodom* and *Justine*, two novels featuring graphic violence, cruelty and orgiastic sexual excess. These provocative writings helped define sadomasochism or S&M, as well as influencing film, art, theatre and music, giving voice to the darker corners of human desire.

Sexual expression & Victorian repression *1837–1901*

Stereotyped as an age of sexual puritanism, shaped by fears of overpopulation and disease among the working class, sex remained a source of inspiration in theatre, literature and art. Artists like Aubrey Beardsley (p.60) produced highly sexualised, satirical illustrations. Later, collectives like the Bloomsbury Group defied societal norms, using sexual freedom to inform their works.

Freud's *Interpretation of Dreams* & psychoanalysis *1899*

Sigmund Freud revolutionised our understanding of sex, desire and the human mind. The founder of psychoanalysis, Freud believed that unlocking the unconscious mind was key to revealing our deepest, most repressed emotions and desires. Asserting that dreams articulated what our conscious minds could not, Freud's ideas profoundly influenced 20th-century art, philosophy and literature, paving the way for Surrealism's excavation of the erotic unconscious.

Surrealism's erotic journeys into fantasy *post-WWI*

Emerging from the ruins of World War I, the Surrealists were a group of artists and writers who used their artwork to explore and express the unconscious mind. Through dreamlike scenes and strange, uncanny imagery, the Surrealists used techniques like automatic drawing and writing to reveal hidden desires. Artists like Dalí (p.76), Magritte (p.86) and Fini (p.82) channelled their deepest fears and desires, infusing their fantastical work with intense sexual tension.

The Women's Liberation Movement *1960s*

In the 1960s, a wave of feminist intellectualism emerged across Europe and the US, challenging misogyny and advocating for women's rights, highlighted by the first National Women's Liberation Conference held in New York in 1968. Artists like Lee Lozano (p.94) and Judy Chicago (p.106) responded by centring their own bodies and sexual experiences in their work. Their confrontational, evocative erotic art sought to break free from the male gaze and reclaim female autonomy and expression.

Body politics & the Civil Rights Act *1960s*

The Civil Rights Movement fought to end racism and segregation in the US. Led by grassroots organisations, activists, scholars and ordinary citizens, it secured vital legal protections for the civil rights of all Americans, emboldening a new wave of artists like Ana Mendieta, Jean-Michel Basquiat and Mickalene Thomas, who spotlighted race, sexuality and body politics in their work. Mickalene Thomas in particular redefined beauty standards, portraying Black women in empowered, sensual poses that celebrated self-ownership.

Radical intimacies in queer art *1960s*

The 1960s also marked a significant turning point for the LGBTQ+ community, with the partial decriminalisation of same-sex activity in Europe and the US in 1967. This shift allowed individuals to express their identities and relationships openly. While queer erotic art has existed for centuries, artists like Tom of Finland (p.98) and Andy Warhol could create without fear of censorship, sharing their work widely and celebrating queer intimacy.

Transgressive performance art *1980s*

As personal freedoms expanded alongside technological advances and globalisation, performance art emerged as a vital medium to express anxieties, fears and radical politics. Artists like Marina Abramović (p.108) and Yoko Ono used their bodies as sites for erotic expression and transgressive experimentation. Similarly, figures like Vito Acconci and, later, Ron Athey (p.122), pushed boundaries through their provocative performances.

The Young British Artists *1990s*

Known as the YBAs, the Young British Artists were the *enfants terribles* of the British art scene. Coming to prominence in the 1990s, many of these artists – like Tracey Emin (p.114) and Sarah Lucas (p.112) – studied, worked and lived together. Creating satirical, Pop-adjacent art that reflected the turbulence of their everyday lives, they brought a candid, often irreverent approach to sex, which became a central theme to their work.

Erotic art today *2020s*

Erotic art remains a rich site for experimentation, research and activism. By engaging with ongoing debates around race, class and gender, it often highlights the identities and experiences of marginalised communities amid a resurgence of conservative attitudes towards sexual expression. More recently, the relaunched art and literary journal *Erotic Review* serves as a platform for modern audiences to explore desire. Collaborations among sex workers, artists and performers are also creating works that blur the lines between film, art and pornography, with groups like Four Chambers using art history to inform their filmmaking.

Key Terms

Abstraction
Emerging in Europe in the early 20th century, this style plays with shape and colour, prioritising feelings over reality – expressing emotions rather than mimicking life.

Art Brut
Coined by the artist Jean Dubuffet, *Art Brut* translates as 'Raw Art' and describes art outside the academic traditions, embracing folk art, graffiti and outsider art – spontaneous, unpolished work from society's fringes.

Automatism
Art-making process tapping into the unconscious mind via techniques like automatic drawing or free association, embracing spontaneity to produce work that is authentic and revealing.

Avant-garde
A French term embodying the bold belief that art can spark societal change, describing artworks considered radical, pushing the boundaries of politics and ideas.

Bacchanalia
Ancient Roman festival honouring Bacchus (god of wine, known to the Greeks as Dionysus) with wild drinking, dancing and rituals. Now describes any raucous, wine-fuelled celebration.

Bestiality
Sexual intercourse between a human and animal, highly taboo in most cultures.

Bloomsbury group
An early 20th-century collective of writers, artists and critics living in Bloomsbury in London. Rebelling against the stifling societal and artistic norms of the era, they embraced Modernist ideas and radical ways of living.

Body politics
The investigation of how bodies are included or excluded in political, social or cultural contexts, shedding light on how bodies are depicted, and what this says about society.

Classicism
Drawing inspiration from the arts and cultures of ancient Greece and Rome, Classicism celebrated proportion and

harmony, with artworks that focused on creating realistic depictions of the natural, human form.

Composition
The arrangement of figurative or abstract elements in an artwork to create a sense of harmony or balance. Artists have historically used geometry to create ideal compositions.

Dada
A post-WWI 'anti-art' movement embracing absurdity, nonsense and satire, rebelling against traditional art and society's conventions.

Expressionism
An emotional powerhouse of a movement born in late 19th-century Germany, conveying deep feelings and spiritual themes through vibrant colour, dynamic movement and distorted forms that defy conventions.

Feminism
First emerging in 18th century Europe, feminism is the socio-political movement advocating for equality between the sexes. The ideology encompasses the quest for political, economic, personal and social rights.

Figurative Art
Shining a light on real-world subjects, especially people. In stark contrast to Abstraction, figurative art communicates the human experience in a realistic style.

Fetish
A form of sexual desire, fixation or compulsion linking pleasure and gratification to an object, activity or body part beyond the typical sexual organs – feet, for instance.

Freudian
Referring to the theories of the 19th-century psychoanalyst, Sigmund Freud. This term is often used in reference to human sexuality and the unconscious mind, exploring the intricate layers of our behaviour and desires.

French Revolution
A period of political upheaval (1789–99) that reshaped France, featuring revolutionary wars and the execution of ruling elite, including King Louis XVI.

Kamasutra
An ancient Indian Hindu Sanskrit text offering wisdom on relationships and pleasure, exploring the philosophy and theory of love.

Kink
Unconventional sexual practices, concepts or fantasies, originating from the idea of a 'bend' in sexual behaviour that deviates from the norm.

Male gaze
Coined by the theorist Laura Mulvey, the term relates to the depiction of women as sexual objects from a male perspective, often catering for the desires of a cisgender, heterosexual male viewer.

Modernism
A sweeping philosophical movement that peaked in the mid-20th century. It reflects the rapid changes brought about by industrialisation and globalisation, capturing the complexities of an increasingly fraught, but technologically advanced, world.

Mysticism
The belief or experience of becoming one with God, or the 'Absolute'. In the medieval age, mysticism also referred to the ecstatic, altered states of consciousness when connecting with the divine.

Pop Art
A vibrant movement inspired by consumer culture, turning everyday objects into art. It thrived in the 1950s–60s, especially in the US and UK.

Psychoanalysis
Invented by Sigmund Freud to explore the relationship between the conscious and unconscious mind. Unlocking repressed fears, emotions and desires using techniques such as dream interpretation and free association.

Renaissance
Beginning in 15th-century Florence and inspired by the art and literature of ancient Greece and Rome, it aimed to revive idealism and beauty in art. Focused on mythological and religious themes, figures were depicted with stunning realism and intricate detail.

Sadism
The feeling of pleasure derived from causing physical or

psychological pain. Named after the notorious Marquis de Sade, whose provocative works explored transgressive themes, this term delves into the psychology of dominance and control.

Salon
Official French exhibitions later synonymous with prestigious shows. These were often conservative, sparking avant-garde movements like the *Salon des Refusés*.

Sadomasochism
Sadism and masochism, collectively known as sadomasochism, is the feeling of pleasure received from either inflicting or receiving pain or humiliation.

Scylla
A multi-headed, man-eating sea monster from Greek mythology, feared by sailors navigating narrow straits near Charybdis.

Sheela-na-Gig
Medieval stone carvings of nude women with exaggerated vulvas, often found on Norman or Romanesque churches. Their meaning remains a mystery.

Shunga
A Japanese term that translates literally as 'Spring' – a euphemism for sex. Shunga typically refers to Japanese erotic woodblock prints or hand-painted scrolls.

Submission
Typified by one sexual partner taking on a more dominant, authoritative role, often exerting control, while the other partner embraces obedience.

Surrealism
Founded in the 1920s by André Breton, the Surrealists sought to explore the unconscious mind, producing uncanny artworks filled with hidden symbols.

Contributors

Elise Bell is an arts writer and commentator based in London. She has been published in *The Financial Times*, the *Independent*, the *Guardian*, *Dazed* and *GQ*.

Hoxton Mini Press is a small independent publisher from east London. Independent… Yes! We believe in books. We believe in beautiful books. We believe in beautiful books that you collect and put on nice wooden shelves and keep for future generations. We also plant loads of trees.

About this book

In an age when everything can be researched online we believe that strong opinion is better than excessive information. Showcasing works by artists who captured pivotal moments of eroticism, each piece tells a unique story of erotic expression. This guide aspires to ignite your curiosity, encouraging deeper exploration into the rich tapestry of erotic art.

Artworks

UNKNOWN ARTIST

The Venus of Willendorf, c. 25,000 BCE

An erotic mystery yet to be deciphered

The *Venus of Willendorf* has always been shrouded in mystery. Created around 25,000 BCE and unearthed in 1908 in a Palaeolithic site in Austria, the Venus is a female figure, her body nude and her breasts engorged. With its exaggerated sexual features, art historians initially presumed the figure was an early ode to fertility, but it has since become an enigma. Lacking a visible face, the head reveals an intricate pattern of beads, perhaps a headdress. Could this early Venus have been a goddess? A deity to an ancient and perfect femininity? Others argue that the strange proportions reveal an early self-portrait – women looking down and depicting their own bodies from above. Looking at the Venus today encourages us to participate in a collective act of time travel: the hands that tenderly formed the tiny figurine unknowingly preserved one of the earliest traces of eroticism to art history. Though answers of any kind are buried deep within our Earth's past, the *Venus of Willendorf* has become shorthand for unruly beauty: a paean to the sensuality of the female form.

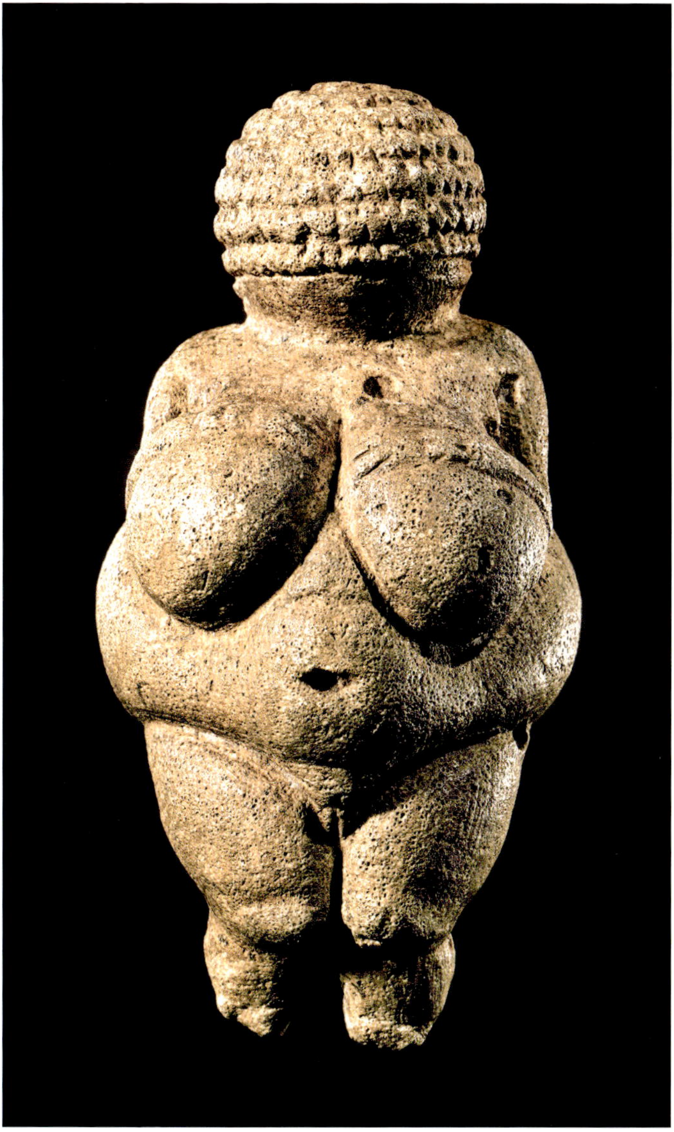

The Venus of Willendorf, c. 25,000 BCE, limestone coloured with red ochre, 11.1 cm height, Naturhistorisches Museum Wien

THE SHUVALOV PAINTER

Oinochoe, c. 430–420 BCE

Time-defying tenderness

This small, glossy clay jug is a perfect example of the ancient Greek tradition of red-figure pottery. Found in the Italian town of Locri in southern Italy, the jug has been attributed to the artist known as the Shuvalov Painter, a prolific ceramicist who ran a workshop in Athens at the time. Erotic scenes were a common motif in ancient Greek art, with sex a central part of public life. In this scene, a man and a woman, most likely a sex worker from a brothel, are caught in the immediate prelude to sexual intercourse. In this gap between intent and action there is a palpable erotic tension, the viewer able to project their fantasy of what is to come, the sexual act existing as yet only in our imaginations. Yet there's something tender, even moving; the gentle placement of her hands on his shoulders, as if to steady herself, the fumbling awkwardness of the scene as he waits for her. It's a crystal-clear depiction of relationships that feel close to our own, even if separated by several millennia. This familiarity is the real site of the erotic – not just the sexual encounter being shown, but the proximity of this image to an eternal human experience.

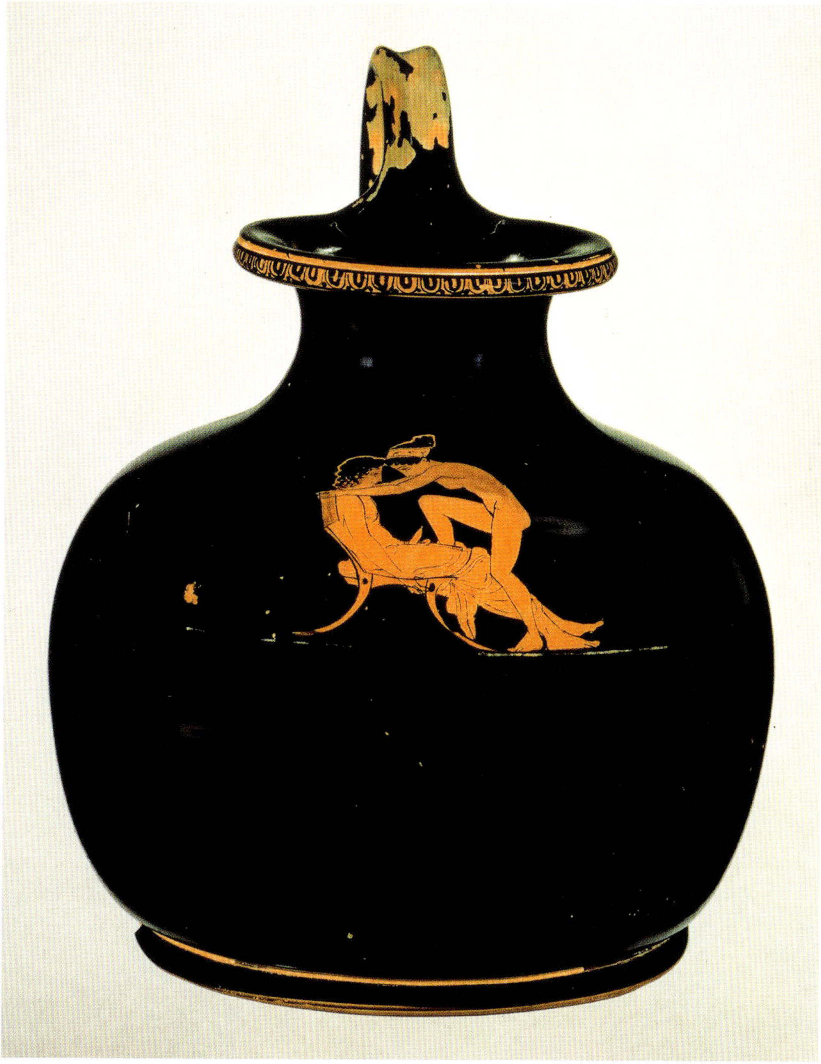

The Shuvalov Painter, *Oinochoe*, c. 430–420 BCE, pottery, 19 × 15.5 cm, Antikensammlung Berlin

UNKNOWN ARTIST

A love-making scene, Sunga Dynasty, c. 1st century BCE

The circle of life

Believed to be inspired by the *Kamasutra*, this plaque, made from bone and created around the 1st century BCE during the Shunga period, is a fine example of how central erotic art and the teachings of the *Kamasutra* were to Hindu culture, inspiring artists and craftsman in ancient India and beyond. Often mischaracterised in the West solely as a 'sex manual', the *Kamasutra* is a rich philosophical text describing how to live a good and gracious life – from managing a household to supporting and sexually gratifying a partner. With 'Kama' translating as sensual pleasure and 'Sutra' meaning thread or line, the text places libido and sexuality as one of the most sacred driving forces in life. In this highly decorative and ornate scene, a figure penetrates another, their legs spread wide and arms around another third figure. This smaller figure could be a child, the image a teaching-tool or a symbol for how sex is the genesis of procreation and family-making. As lucidly depicted here, sexual pleasure is the vital component in the creation of human life.

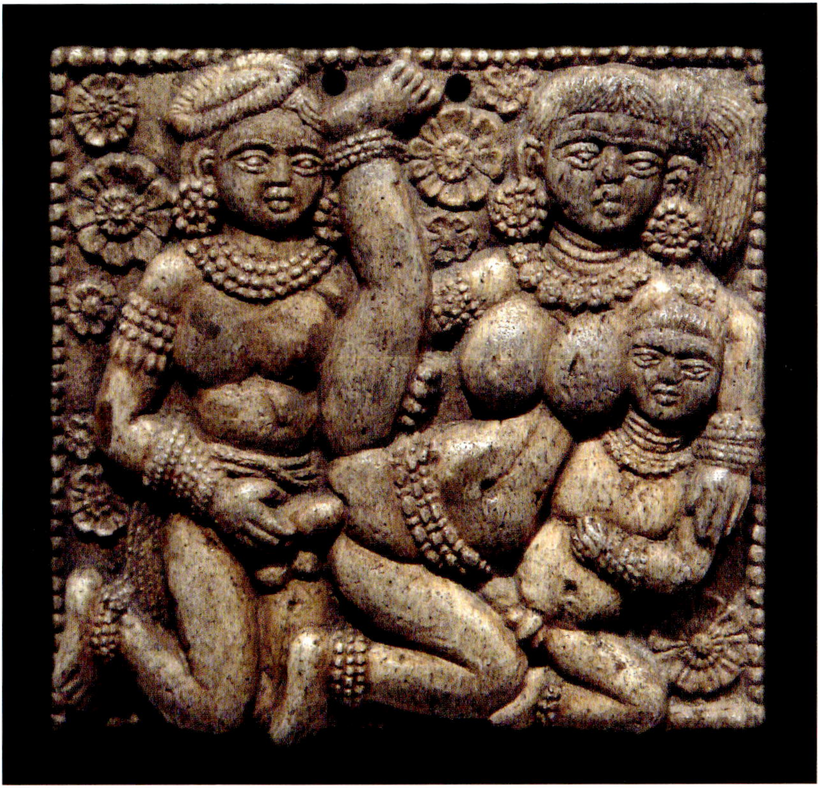

India / Bangladesh: A love-making scene, Sunga Dynasty, 1st century BCE, bone, 5.5 cm × 5.7 cm

UNKNOWN ARTIST

Roman fresco from the suburban baths in Pompeii, c. 62–79 CE

Secrets of the bathhouse

In Ancient Greece and Rome, sex and pleasure lived side-by-side with daily life. The sexual exploits of Greco-Roman gods and demi-gods were openly shared and celebrated, allowing for the public discussion and portrayal of sexuality and intercourse. In Pompeii, traces of these attitudes can be found among the city ruins; the apocalyptic eruption of Mount Vesuvius in 79 CE killed around 10,000 residents and submerged the city in a blanket of ash, coating priceless mosaics, artworks and even human remains in a protective layer, creating an eerie tableaux of a society frozen in time. In the remains of a suburban bathhouse, a fresco depicts cunnilingus. A man is shown crouching on the floor as a woman, holding up her right leg, receives oral pleasure. There are a few theories as to why this, and many other frescoes like it, appear in the suburban baths, with some historians suggesting it might advertise a brothel on the upper floor. That the male figure is clothed and the female figure naked applies credence to this theory, but the overall picture it evokes is more importantly one of openness – an openness to the realities of sex, and sex work, co-existing among the mundanity of the leisure class.

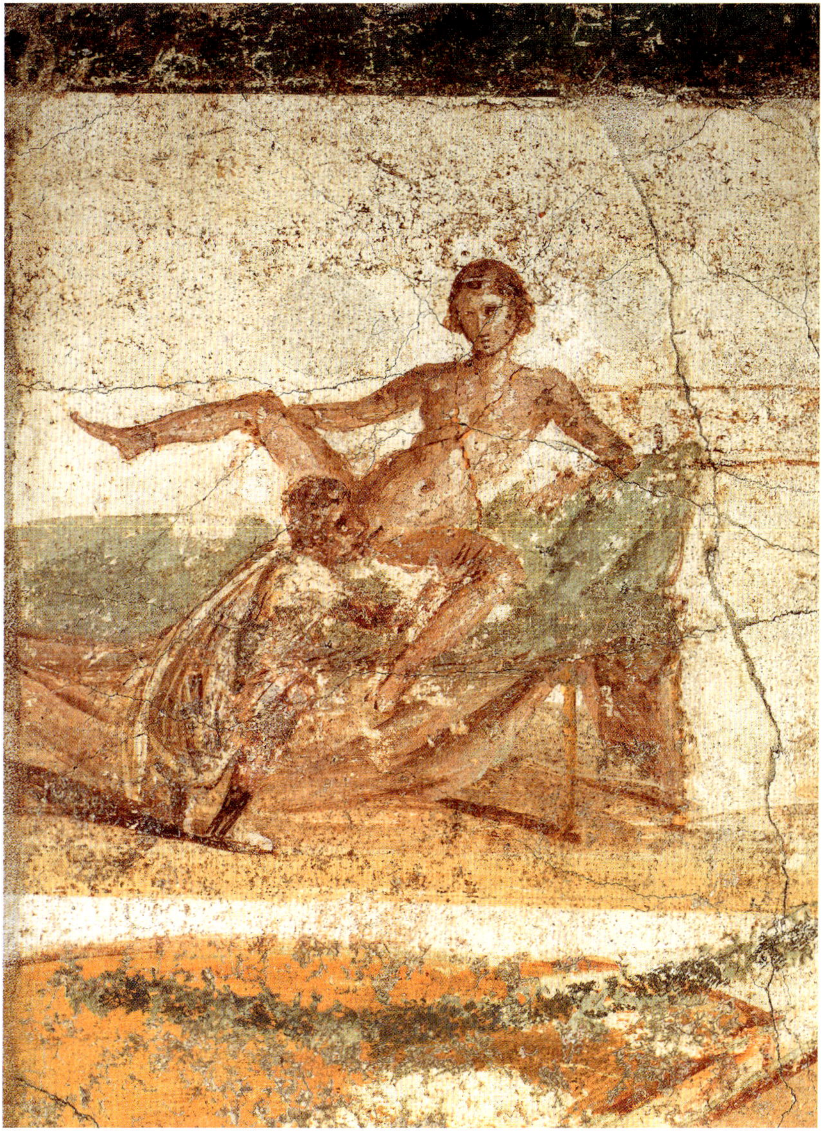

Roman fresco from the suburban baths in Pompeii, c. 62–79 CE

UNKNOWN ARTIST

The Khajuraho temples c. 11th century

Sacred orgy carved in stone

In India's Chhatarpur district, almost 400 miles southeast of New Delhi, are some of the world's most important works of erotic art: the Khajuraho temples. Built during the Chandelas dynasty between 970–1030, the temples belonged to two different religions – Hinduism and Jainism – and were created as religious offerings and as a site where pilgrims could congregate. Sex – and a healthy, fulfilling erotic life – were central to worship in both religions, with the life-giving potential of sexual union seen as a sacred act. Artistic reliefs of sexual passion were not uncommon. In this figurative relief, couples engage in rapturous intercourse as onlookers watch from either side. Though making up only ten per cent of the figurative reliefs on the temples, the frenetic, propulsive motion of these erotic figures, some fornicating, others licking, sucking or fondling one another, creates a sense of divine rhythm, the temple complex thrillingly alive despite its stone facade. Almost one thousand years later, the Khajuraho temples have become a World Heritage Site, these reliefs celebrating an ancient understanding between two religions, as well as the sacred power of the erotic.

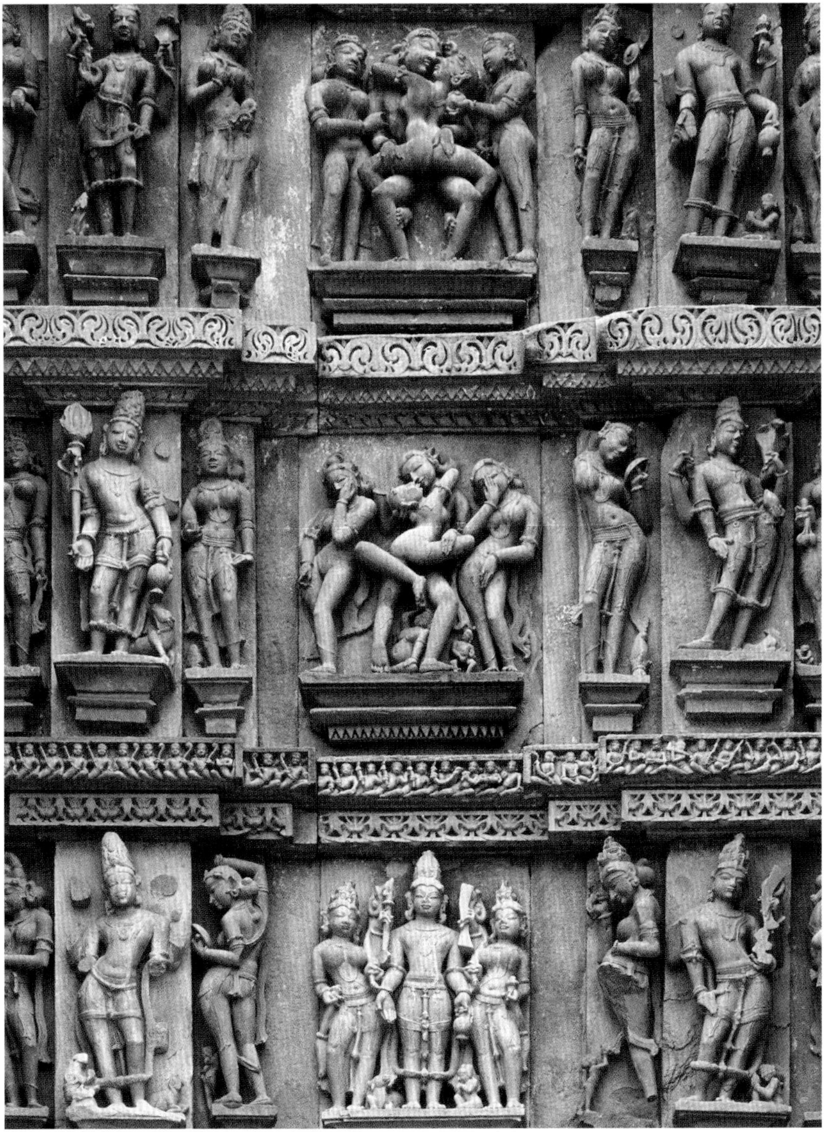

Figurative relief from the Khajuraho temples, Ornate statues on two or three tiers on Vishwanath temple, c. 11th century, stone carvings, Madhya Pradesh

UNKNOWN ARTIST

Kilpeck Sheela-na-Gig, c. 12th century

A Middle Age peek-a-boo

Set within the lush rolling hills of Hereford is a small, 12th-century church in the village of Kilpeck. A picture-postcard scene, the church was ornately decorated by early craftspeople, the door alone including elements of Viking, Celtic and Saxon design. Adorned with 89 handcrafted corbels (wall supports), you might initially miss the small figure impishly showcasing an enlarged vulva between its legs. But once you see the Kilpeck Sheela-na-Gig, it is difficult to forget. This is one of the most famous examples of a Sheela-na-Gig – a carving of a nude woman displaying an exaggerated vulva, typically found in Ireland, the UK, France and Spain. Historians have long debated their origins and purpose. Some argue that these figures, with their grotesque features and gargoyle-like positioning, signify sinful femininity and the corrupting power of lust. Others, that they represent a pre-Christian goddess of fertility, and were created to bring good fortune, or ward off dangerous spirits. Though their original meaning has been lost, the Sheela-na-Gig represents a version of eroticism in both the civic and sacred realms, showing how, even in the most tranquil and arcadian of landscapes, eroticism lurks.

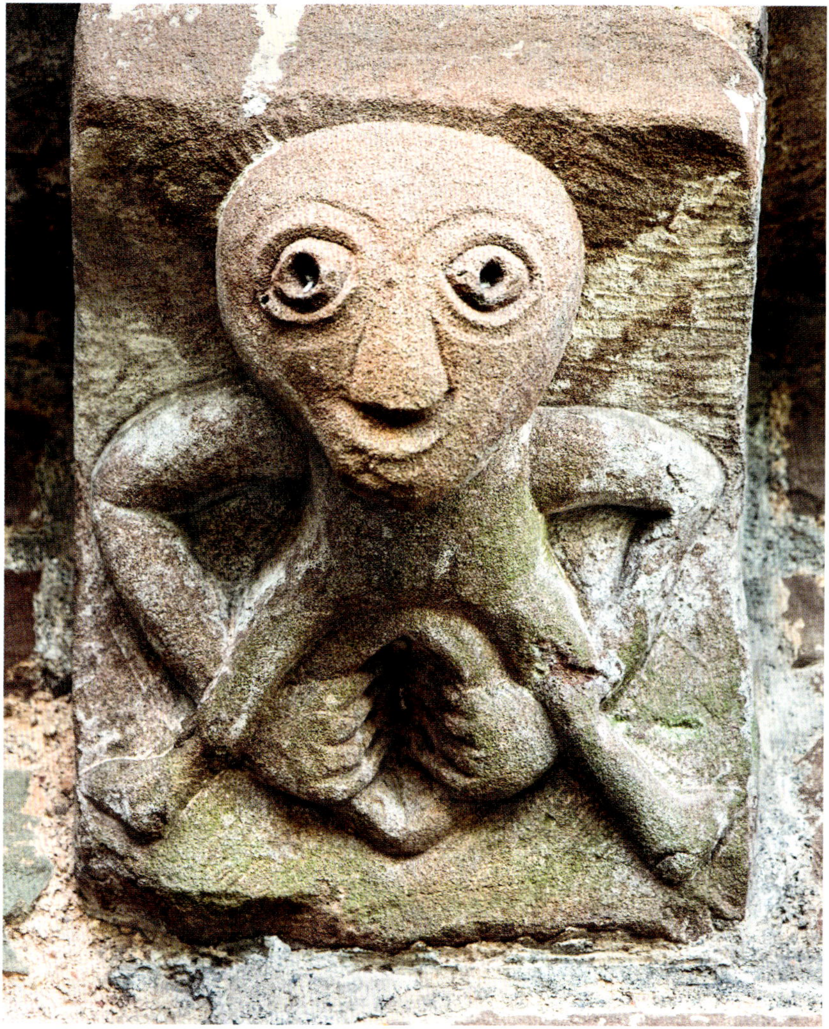

Kilpeck Sheela-na-Gig, c. 12th century, stone, 37.2 × 23 cm,
Church of St Mary and St David, Kilpeck

JEAN LE NOIR

Christ's Side Wound, Prayer Book of Bonne de Luxembourg, c. 1349

Spiritual openings

Rendered in ink, vellum and goldleaf, this small, illuminated religious manuscript was designed for Bonne of Luxembourg, a Bohemian princess living in the 14th century. Perhaps surprisingly, nestled within its pages is an arresting piece of erotic art history. At its centre is a striking depiction of one of Christ's holy wounds: a wide, almond shape outlined in thick, deep crimson that draws the eye in. If you're thinking, *Does that look like…?* you're not alone – but considering the historical context can help to shed some light. Medieval mysticism flourished in this period, positioning Christ's body as a source of divine love in writing and art, as well as an erotic site with readers kissing and touching the pages of manuscripts. Of course, in Catholic dogma, Christ's body also provides literal nourishment; worshippers take into their mouth his body (bread) and blood (wine). This nourishment and life-giving enjoy a close association with the vagina: the site from which life is created and delivered. These symbolic strands meet in this manuscript centerpiece, which offers a glimpse into how the sacred and erotic coexisted.

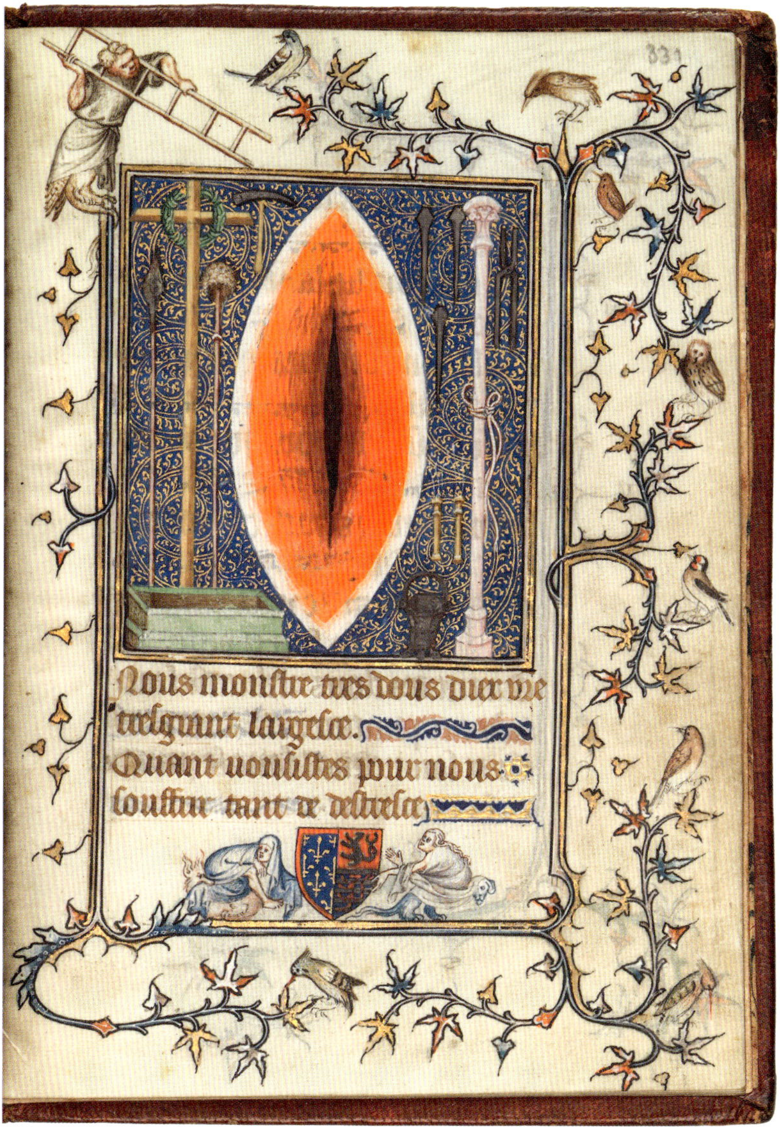

Attributed to Jean Le Noir, *Christ's Side Wound and Instruments of the Passion*, c. 1349, folio 331r, in the *Prayer Book of Bonne of Luxembourg*, The Metropolitan Museum of Art

AFTER MICHELANGELO

Leda and the Swan, after 1530

A fine-feathered friend

One of the most famous lost artworks of the Western canon, Michelangelo's *Leda and the Swan* exists only as a replica. Yet the power of Michelangelo's original work has become legend, with art historian Peter Fuller detailing how a minister of King Louis XIII of France burnt the image due to its 'dangerous obscenity'. It's easy to see why *Leda and the Swan* courted such extreme reactions. The image depicts the sexually relentless king of the gods Jupiter, who, after spying on the beautiful Leda, transforms into a swan. Throwing himself into her arms and feigning innocence, Jupiter seduces Leda on the banks of the river. Michelangelo's image radiates erotic charge: the swan's slender, phallic neck rests between Leda's breasts, his uplifted beak gently touching her lips. There's also the swan's tail, which seems to press between Leda's legs. Leda too looks fatigued, her head drooping as if in defeat, her limbs entangled with the swan. As powerful as this eroticism is, it also speaks to themes of subjugation, coercion and domination, Jupiter preying on Leda's vulnerability. A rape fantasy in feathers? The work remains potent to this day.

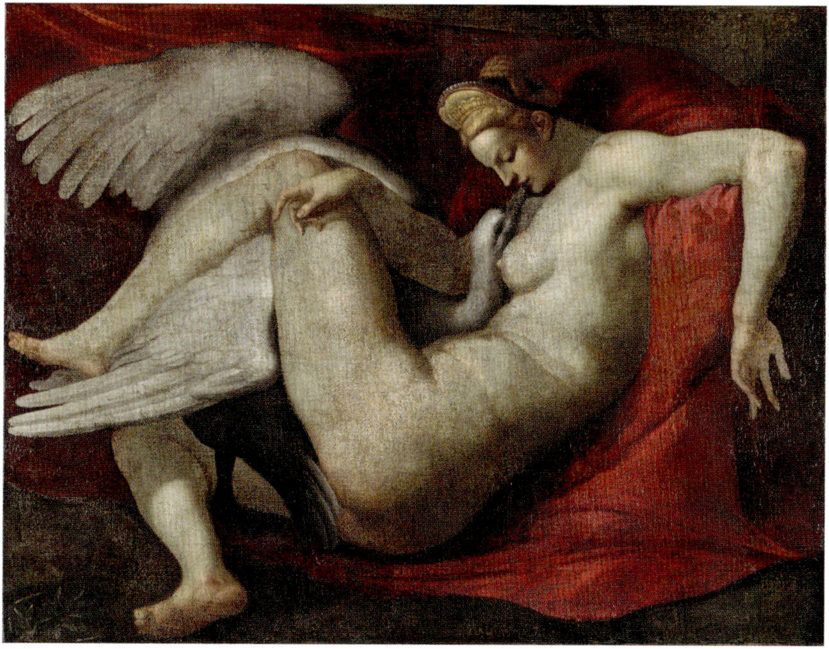

After Michaelangelo, *Leda and the Swan*, after 1530, oil on canvas, 105.4 × 141 cm, copy held by The National Gallery

TITIAN

Venus of Urbino, 1538

Beauty behind the curtain

Titian's sensual *Venus of Urbino* might look like a typical nude, but the boldness of her steady gaze meeting our own suggests something altogether more radical. Some believe the painting's subject was the Venetian courtesan Zafetta; others argue it was a wedding present commissioned by the Duke of Urbino. There are a few clues backing the second theory: a servant rifles through a chest of drawers (or what could be a marriage trousseau) in the corner. A dog sleeping at her feet could symbolise fidelity. There's also the placement of her hands: it's unclear whether she is protecting her modesty or caressing herself – it's interesting to note that it was then believed women could only conceive if they reached orgasm. This imbues the painting with a thrilling erotic tension, our Venus becoming a symbol of lust and the ownership of one's sexuality. Were this Venus modelled after the Duchess of Urbino herself, it's likely the painting would have been hidden behind a silk cloth, shielded from everyday viewing and unveiled only for prestigious guests: Earls, Counts – even Popes. Whoever this Venus really was, Titian provided a masterful glimpse into the Renaissance's erotic psyche, revealing impulses not unlike our own.

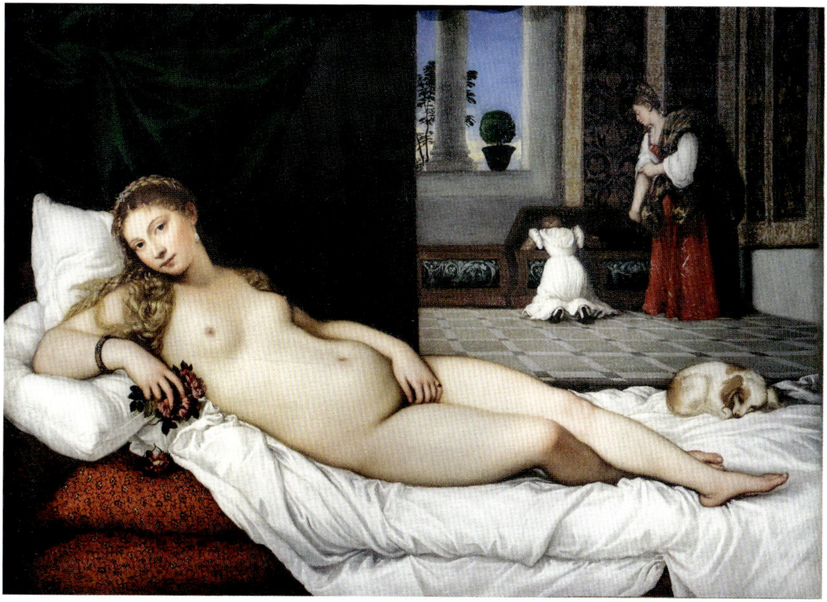

Titian, *Venus of Urbino*, 1538, oil on canvas, 119 × 165 cm, Uffizi Gallery

FRANCISCO DE ZURBARÁN

Agnus Dei, c. 1635–1640

Submission – Spanish Baroque style

In this tender depiction of a young ram trussed and waiting upon a table, Francisco de Zubarán's *Agnus Dei* expresses the allure of total surrender. 'Behold, the Lamb of God, who takes away the sins of the world!' – so proclaims St John the Baptist upon seeing Jesus. Countless painters have been inspired by the sacrificial lamb as a symbol for Christ, and themes of annihilation and submission permeate the artworks of the Baroque and Renaissance period. In Catholicism, the boundaries between the sacred and the sexual have often been porous, with women claiming to have entered into 'divine love' or a holy marriage with the Lord, and mediaeval monks writing of Christian mystics that received highly sensual, orgiastic visions of Christ. There are clear power dynamics at play here, namely the dominating force of religion evoking a sensual desire to submit. We're not suggesting you look at this lamb and consider it 'sexy', but the role it occupies is marked by this very desire: the lamb becomes a symbol of submission incarnate. In presenting an image of pure devotion, de Zubarán touches on something carnal.

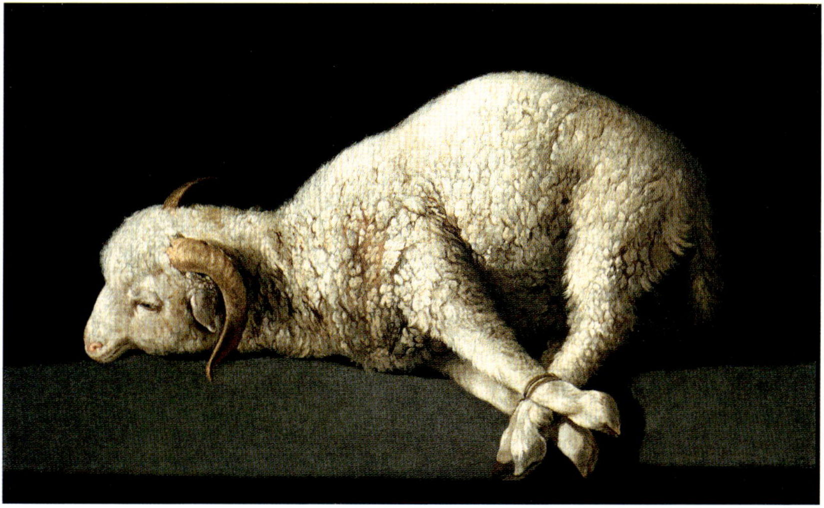

Francisco de Zurbarán, *Agnus Dei*, c. 1635–1640, oil on canvas, 38 × 62 cm, Museo del Prado

GIAN LORENZO BERNINI

Ecstasy of St Teresa, 1647–52

Catholic rapture rendered in marble

More than just an altarpiece, Bernini's *Ecstasy of Saint Teresa* has come to evoke the erotic possibilities of religious art. Completed in 1652, the *Ecstasy* was designed for the Cornaro Chapel in Rome and depicts the moment when the Carmelite nun encountered the holy spirit. Described in her writing as an arrow 'thrusting' in and out of her heart, the love of God pierces her entrails, leaving Teresa in '[a] pain so great that it made me moan; and yet so surpassing was the sweetness of this excessive pain, that I could not wish to be rid of it.' Bernini renders this moment in exquisite detail, as a clothed Teresa seems to swoon, her mouth open as if in climax, in a sigh of sublime pleasure as a cherubic angel points his arrow towards her. Art historians have highlighted the sculpture's clear eroticism, with mystical unions as described by Teresa often involving sexual or pleasurable encounters with the divine. Not pictured here, this scene is further intensified by two patron portraits just beyond the altarpiece looking on as if from the balcony of a theatre, making Teresa's ecstasy a literal erotic spectacle.

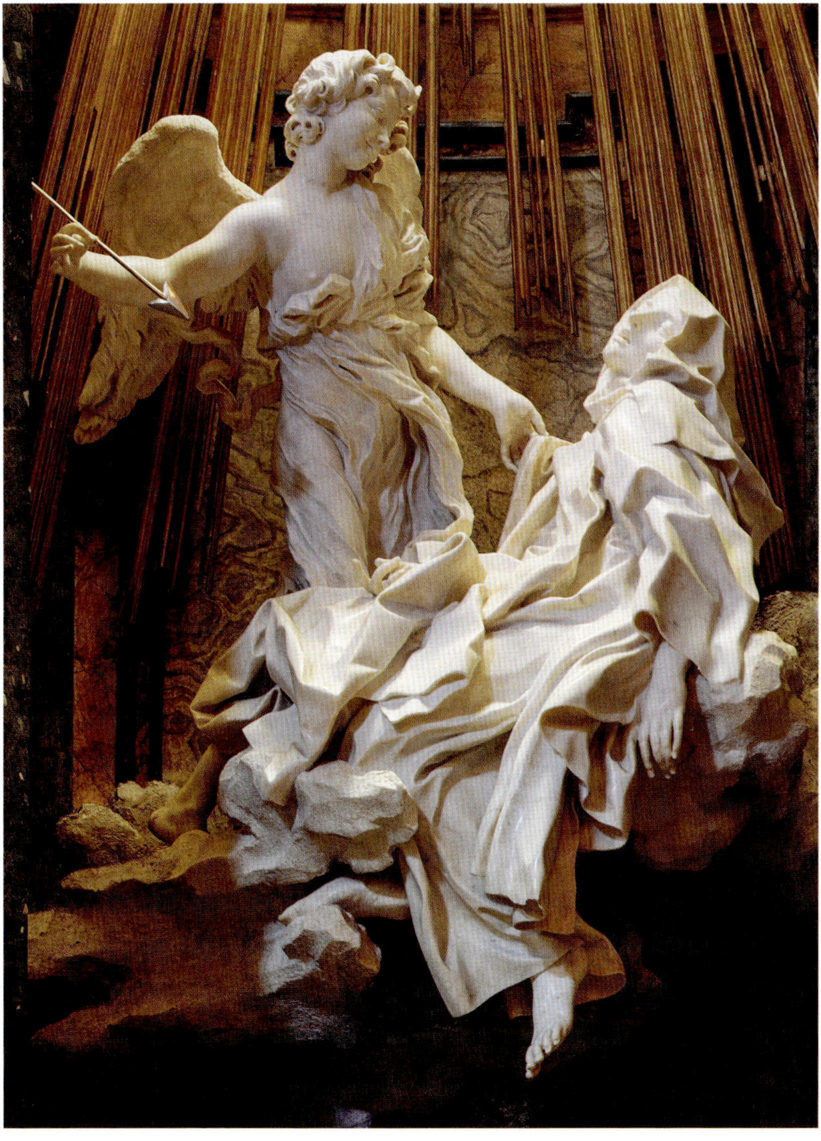

Gian Lorenzo Bernini, *Ecstasy of St Teresa*, 1647–52, marble, life-size, Santa Maria della Vittoria

FRANCESCO SALVIATI

The Triumph of the Phallus, c. 17th century

Bacchanalian festivities

Deep in the archives of the British Museum, you may come across an engraving made from an original drawing by Francesco Salviati. A portraitist to some of the most elite families of Renaissance Italy, Salviati also trained his hand on scenes of a more erotic nature. *The Triumph of the Phallus* contains a highly detailed engraving of a Bacchanalia or Greek Liberalia. These processions, linked to sexual celebration and the cult of fertility, would see an enormous model phallus paraded through the streets. Locals and religious devotees would join in, frolicking together with uninhibited revelry that would descend into an orgiastic feast of wine, food and other such substances spilling out into the city streets. In Salviati's rendering, beautiful women lead the garlanded phallus, while ahead stands a representation of a vulva, curtains positioned like legs about to be pulled open by young cherubs ready to welcome the phallus. These artistic renderings of paganistic erotic celebration were increasingly popular motifs during the Renaissance – perhaps in response to the comparably repressive attitudes towards sex in the Christian church. Even in the gilded corridors of the Medici's Florence, you'd have been hard-pressed to find such thrilling parties.

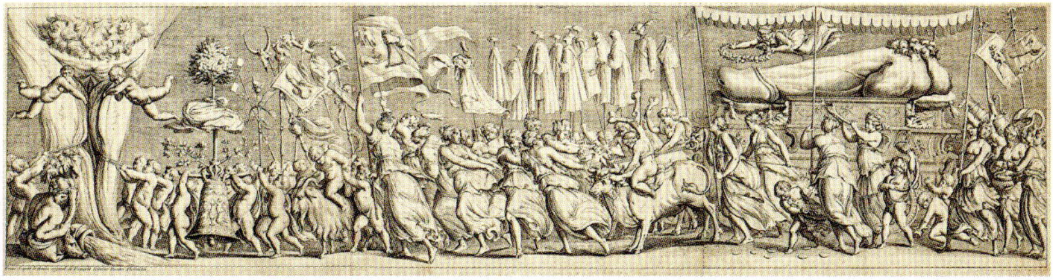

Francesco Salviati, *The Triumph of the Phallus*, c. 17th century, etching on paper, 39.4 × 161 cm, The British Museum

JEAN-HONORÉ FRAGONARD

The Swing, c. 1767–68

Rococo peep show

At first glance, you'd be forgiven for thinking Fragonard's *The Swing* was just a pretty picture. But look closer and you might realise how it became so infamous. Originally commissioned to the historical painter Gabriel François Doyen, he soon proved to be a prude, refusing the request to paint: 'a man's mistress being pushed on a swing by a bishop'. Sensing an opportunity to make his mark, Fragonard stepped in to conjure a Rococo wet dream: a woman dressed in pink silks swinging within a wild, sprawling garden, her lover hiding in the bushes and gazing into her skirts from below. Though we can only imagine what he sees, his adoring face says it all. Meanwhile, in the shadows, an older man (the bishop) manoeuvring the swing looks on – a voyeur to this erotica in Arcadia. The woman's pink satin shoe, having slipped off her foot mid-flight, hangs suspended in the air, and the unkempt, abundant nature of the garden speaks to the abandonment of decency and the painting's wild, untamed expression. What's powerful about the image is not what is shown, but what Fragonard suggests. Is it a paean to the Peeping Tom? Or an ode to female sexuality? It's no wonder the painting was a hit in the French courts.

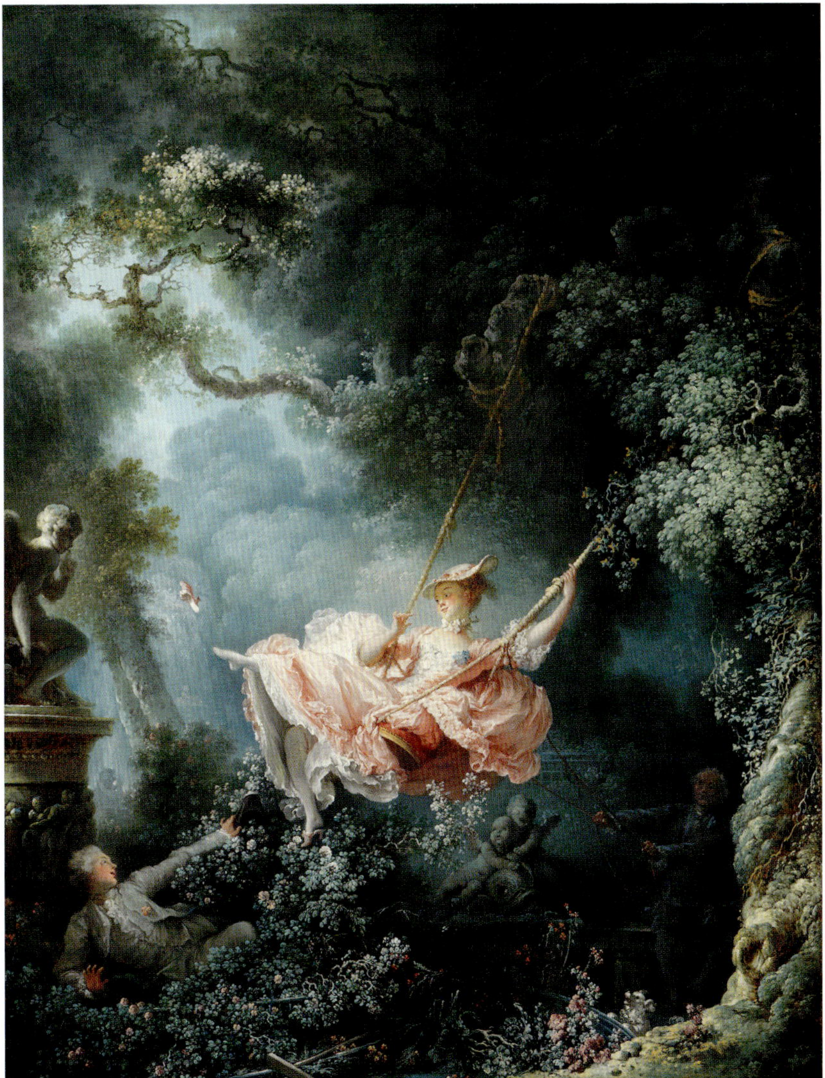

Jean-Honoré Fragonard, *L'Escarpolette (The Swing)*, c. 1767–68,
oil on canvas, 81 × 64.2 cm, The Wallace Collection

The Dream of the Fisherman's Wife, 1814

Slippery fantasy

In 1814, Hokusai published *Kinoe no Komatsu*, a three-volume woodblock-printed tome full of erotic art. Seen by many as the most masterful example of Shunga (shunga meaning 'spring' – a euphemism for sex), it was an erotic offshoot of ukiyo-e, a form of woodblock printing that flourished in Japan's Heian period (794–1185). Though the book included many graphic sexual scenes, one has become legend. *The Dream of the Fisherman's Wife* is Hokusai's evocation of ecstatic abandon: a woman held down, caressed and fondled by two octopuses, the three beings becoming sexually intertwined. The text filling the background details the woman's protests, which include, 'You hateful octopus! Your sucking at the mouth of my womb makes me gasp for breath!' The depiction of bestiality in erotic art has a global precedent, appearing in artworks from the prehistoric era and in the writings of the Marquis de Sade. In the case of Shunga, depictions of human–animal relations were also used to bypass censorship laws. As the woman arches her neck in pleasure, it's clear why this striking image has become so popular within the erotic art canon.

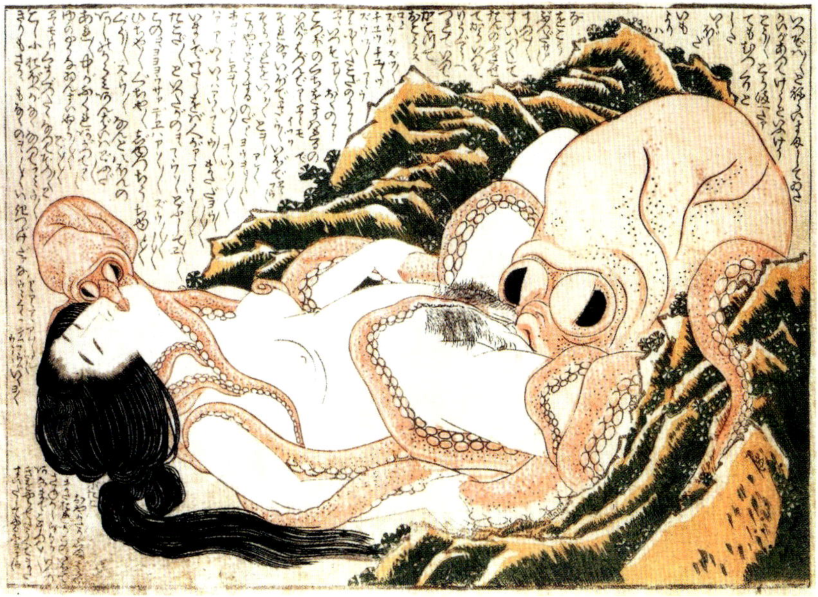

Hokusai, *The Dream of the Fisherman's Wife*, 1814, woodblock print on paper, 19 × 27 cm

RAPHAELLE PEALE

Still Life–A Deception–Venus Rising from a Bath, 1822

What lies beneath

Henry David Thoreau said, 'It's not what you look at that matters, it's what you see.' Depicting a figure hidden behind a *trompe l'oeil* (hyperreal) linen cloth, Peale's *After the Bath* is not about the contents of the image, but what has been concealed. Supposedly created to tease his wife into thinking he had hidden a nude painting behind one of her best napkins, the artist toys with his viewer, suggesting nudity while also erasing it completely. Art historians believe the work was inspired by the 'covered' paintings produced by 18th-century painters, in which nude scenes were suggestively half-concealed by a painted curtain, further amplifying the image's erotic charge. By compelling the viewer to 'complete' the image with their imagination, Peale consciously awakens our fantasies. With one delicate ivory foot peeking out from the bottom and a single outstretched, pale arm holding a clutch of long, golden hair, it recalls biblical narratives such as Susanna and the Elders, in which two patriarchs spy on a bathing Susanna with evil intent. Peale knowingly pushes the viewer into a similar position of lurid voyeur, our imaginations filling in the blank spaces he cannot.

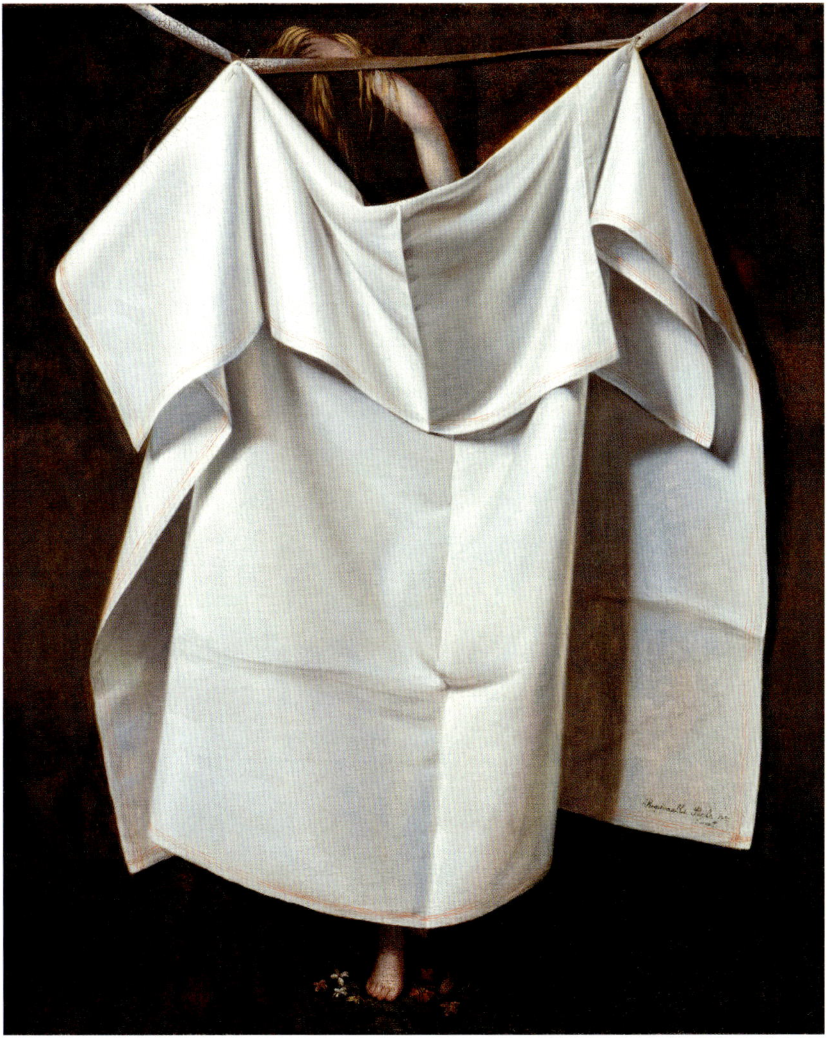

Raphaelle Peale, *Still Life—A Deception—Venus Rising from a Bath*, 1822, oil on canvas, 96.52 × 83.82 × 6.99 cm, The Nelson-Atkins Museum of Art

SARAH GOODRIDGE

Beauty Revealed, 1828

Send nudes

Goodridge's friendship with the politician Daniel Webster reached fever pitch when she sent him a miniature self-portrait of her uncovered breasts. Portrait miniatures had been growing in popularity in the US, the form taking inspiration from eye miniatures (minute paintings of eyes seen and exchanged across Europe). Yet Goodridge's self-portrait goes a step beyond. Set within a six-inch red frame and painted on ivory, a material translucent enough for light to shine through, this miniature glows as if from within. Fuelled by a longing to be seen and desired, Goodridge rendered her breasts swathed in cloth, the rest of her body erased and out of the frame. As small as the painting is, its impact is profound. As a piece of erotic art, it attests to the living, breathing sexuality of women in the 19th century, painting a picture of self-assertion and erotic possibility at a time when women were praised for their submission and modesty. That Webster went on to marry a wealthier, more well-connected woman is beside the point. The real legacy, far outlasting their marriage, is Goodridge's radical use of self-portraiture.

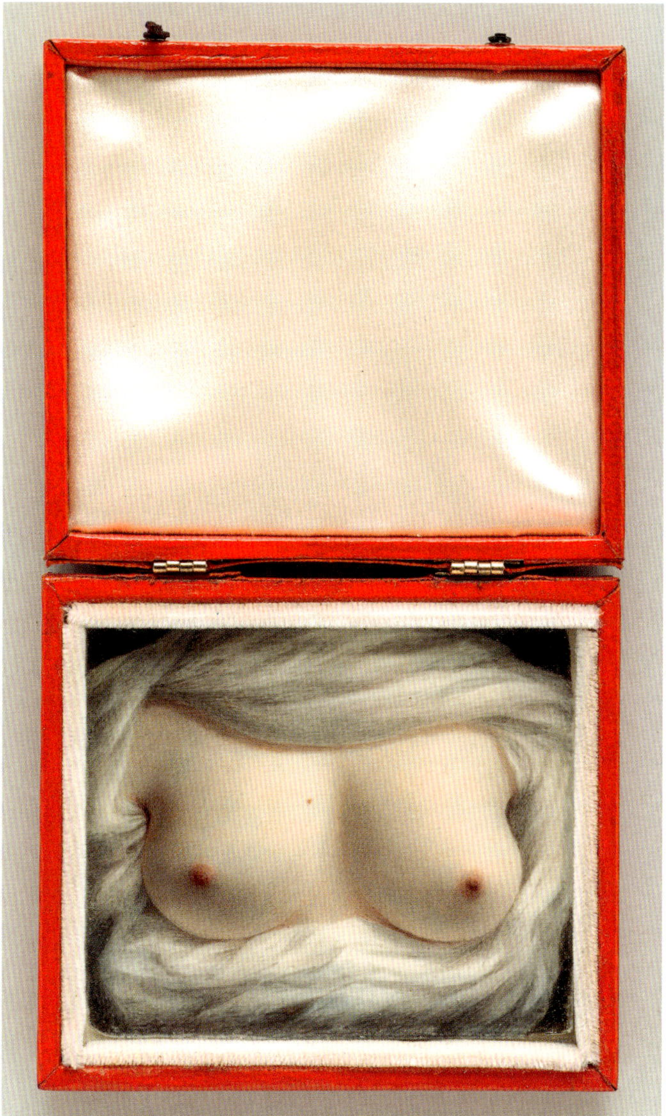

Sarah Goodridge, *Beauty Revealed*, 1828, watercolour on ivory, 6.7 × 8 cm, The Metropolitan Museum of Art

ÉDOUARD MANET

Olympia, 1863

Panic! at the salon

In 1863, Napoleon III received complaints from a number of disgruntled artists whose work had been deemed unfit by the Salon (art exhibitions officially sponsored by the French government). In response, the Emperor created the 'Salon des Refusés' to display the rejected works. One such painting, by Manet, signalled a watershed moment in the history of art. Turning away from the typical 19th-century nudes, which were idealised and protected under the heritage of classicism and mythology, *Olympia* depicts a sex worker reclining on her bed, the nakedness of her body harshly illuminated. Whereas Titian's Venus (p.34) invites the viewer to bed, Manet's Olympia coldly looks on, her hand blocking her sex, her pose stiff and legs crossed – all suggesting that this is a body to be bought. Race is key here, too. Next to Olympia stands her maid, historically neglected from critical appraisal due to her Blackness. Yet, as artist and critic Lorraine O'Grady states, Manet's maid is just as important to the work as Olympia: 'an object to the objectified' the maid is reduced to her race, class and social role – making this an epoch-defining depiction of 19th-century sexual and racial politics. As Émile Zola said: 'When our artists give us Venuses, they correct nature, they lie. Édouard Manet asked himself: Why lie? Why not tell the truth.'

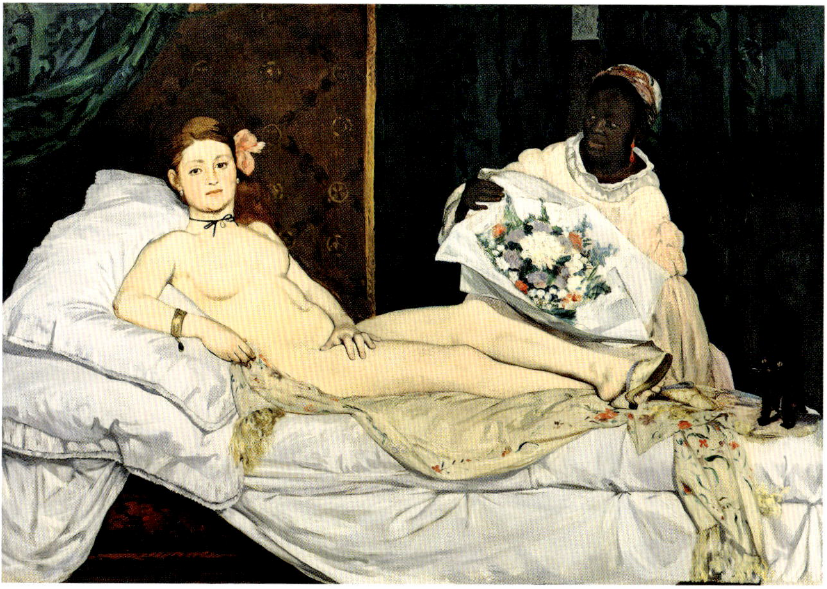

Édouard Manet, *Olympia*, 1863, oil on canvas, 130.5 × 191 cm, Musée d'Orsay

ACHILLE DEVÉRIA

Artist and Sitter, c. 1830–1840

What happens in the studio, stays in the studio

Achille Devéria was born at the right time and in the right place. Studying in Paris, the city that stoked the flames of France's burgeoning liberal sexual mores, Devéria cultivated a glittering career. A talented engraver, he learned from the Old Masters, creating lithographs and watercolour portraits of famous sitters like the French poet Charles Baudelaire. An avowed Libertine, he also chased hedonism and physical pleasure – as hinted at in his erotic engravings and watercolours. With titles befitting a 19th-century Pornhub (*Two Maids and a Donkey*, *Romantic Encounter in a Forest*), Devéria catered to explicit fantasies, using his skill to elevate these visions into fine art. In *Artist and Sitter*, we see a noblewoman pleasuring her portraitist as he returns the favour, using his fingers to stimulate her. It's a scene of reckless abandon in high society, the lovers succumbing to their shared desire. Yet Devéria enhances the image with a striking contrast: to the left of the tryst is the finished portrait, the woman's outwardly respectable appearance watching them coolly. There's a message here: that beneath affected displays of propriety, exists something hungrier and more carnal.

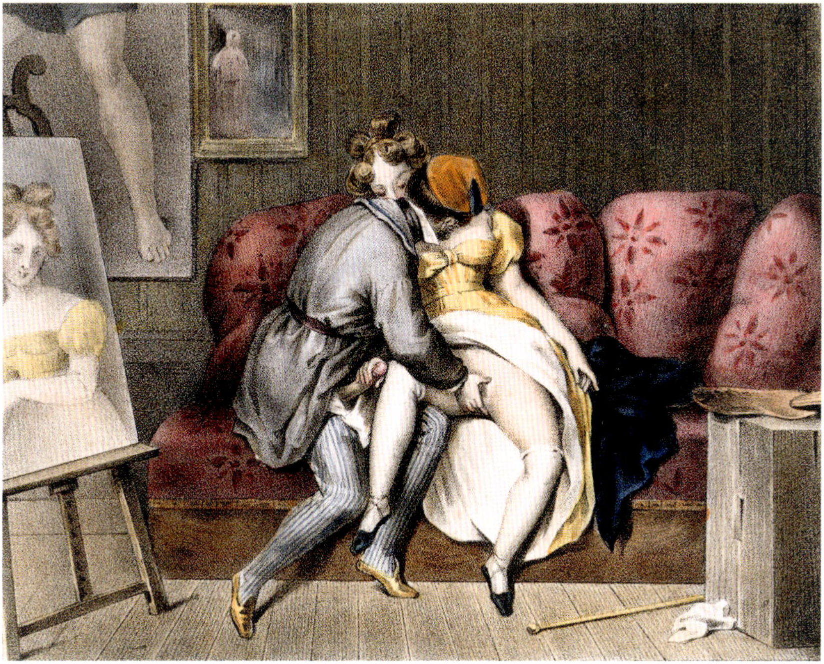

Achille Devéria, *Artist and Sitter: manual foreplay*, c. 1830–1840, colour lithograph

AUGUSTE BELLOC

Untitled c. 1860

Private passions

Little is known about the photographer Auguste Belloc beyond his emotive and human snapshots of erotic life. Hailing from Montrabé in the south of France, Belloc eventually made his way to Paris where he began his artistic career creating miniatures and watercolours before settling as a photographer. Belloc led two important artistic charges, the first of which was the development of colour stereoscopy, a photography technique enhancing the three-dimensional effect by simultaneously presenting two slightly different images – one for each eye. The second was erotic photography. It's this illicit material that cemented Belloc's name in the annals of artistic history, with the artist using this fledgling art form – previously reserved for the rare, official portrait – to create erotic fantasies. Despite most of his works being artificially set in a photographic studio, what makes Belloc's erotic photography so appealing is its humanity. In this image of a half-undressed couple entangled together on a bed, the presence of shoes, stockings and clothing hitched above the hips invokes the breathless and furtive early stages of sex. It's this fumbling, rushed domesticity that makes the image so erotic.

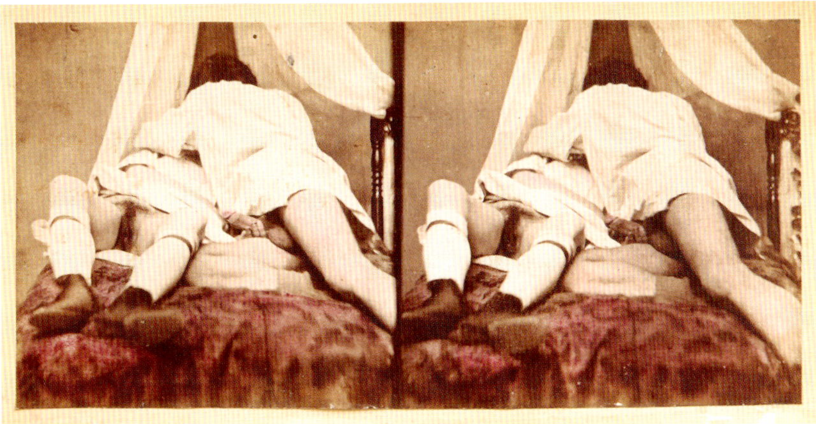

Auguste Belloc, *Untitled*, c. 1860, coloured albumin

GUSTAVE COURBET

The Origin of the World, 1866

Revolution in the salon

In 19th-century Paris, an artistic upheaval was taking place. Led by Gustave Courbet, the Realist movement protested against what they believed to be the sterile nature of Academic painting. By bringing the lives and bodies of the ordinary working class into the artistic sphere, Courbet radically redefined what art could be. When first unveiled, *The Origin of the World* shocked both critics and the public. Framed like a snapshot, *The Origin* depicts a close-up view of a woman lying naked on a bed, her legs parted and her vulva and abdomen bare. Totally disembodied from a face or an identity, the woman becomes a metaphor for all women, her beauty and sex on display. Gone are the hairless, nubile bodies of the Academic tradition: here Courbet is showing womanhood as both coarser and more solid, soft tufts of dark pubic hair encircling her labia. Some argue that this voyeurism is repulsive, women reduced to only what lies between their legs. Yet there's something erotic about the realities of the body – the messy, beautiful, liveliness of sex coming to the forefront. The work remains mired in censorship battles, which suggest Courbet's revolutionary spirit is still very much alive.

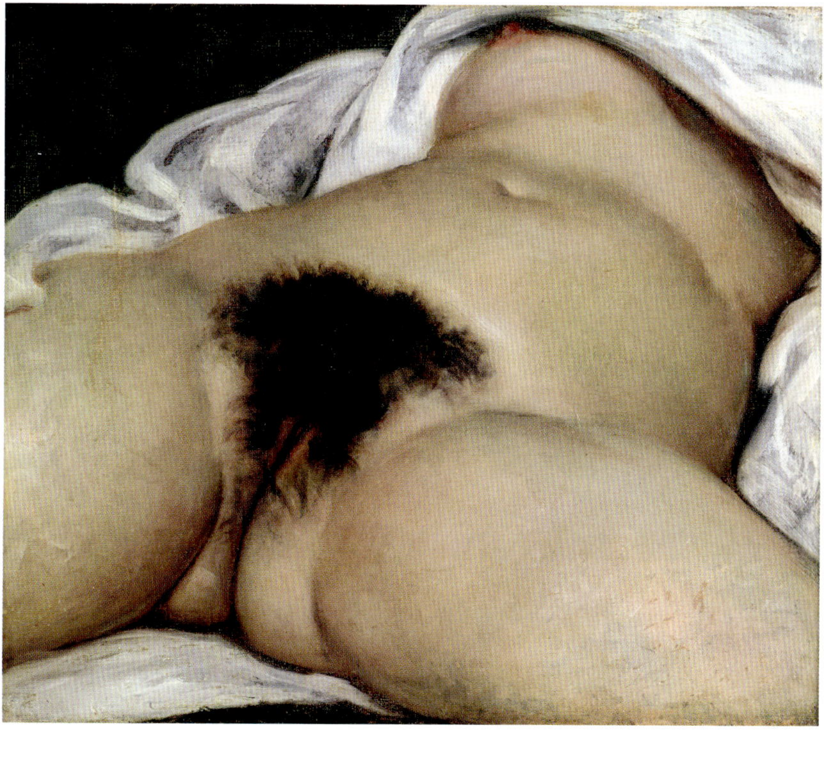

Gustave Courbet, *L'Origine du Monde (The Origin of the World)*, 1866, oil on canvas, 46.3 × 55.4 cm, Musée d'Orsay

HENRI DE TOULOUSE-LAUTREC

In Bed: The Kiss, 1892

Lesbian love in a decadent world

A regular presence in the dancehalls, brothels and absinthe bars that dotted the winding streets of 19th-century Paris, Henri de Toulouse-Lautrec would depict and dedicate his canvases to the twilight characters that frequented that decadent world. It would be easy for his work to slip into a leery voyeurism, but *The Kiss* is both intimate and compassionate. Now sitting pretty in the Musée d'Orsay, Toulouse-Lautrec's seemingly conventional *The Kiss* actually features two women in a brothel, tenderly intertwined beneath a thick duvet. With space at a premium, brothels often saw women sharing beds and naturally becoming close, forging romantic relationships as well as friendships with their bedfellows. Toulouse-Lautrec's impressionistic application of paint imbues the scene with a gauzy, dreamlike quality, the vibrant colour palette vividly capturing a moment of discrete, sensual bliss. In this way, he intertwines the romantic with the erotic. In focusing on the passion between these two women, Toulouse-Lautrec turns what was marginalised and taboo into something universal: the eroticism of the everyday and the joy of sharing a bed with someone you love.

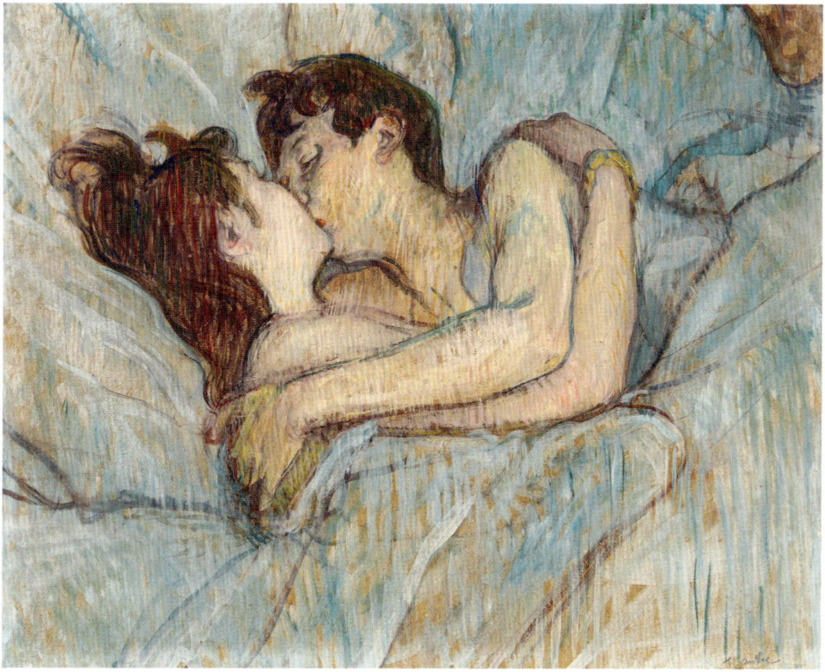

Henri de Toulouse-Lautrec, *Dans le Lit: Le Baiser (In Bed: The Kiss)*, 1892, oil on canvas, 54 × 70 cm, Musée d'Orsay

AUBREY BEARDSLEY

The Lacedaemonian Ambassadors, 1896

Big dick energy

With their stiff upper lips and covered ankles, the Victorians are famous for their repression. But scratch beneath the surface of this outwardly prudish epoch, and you'll find a society fascinated with sex. With his spindly finger firmly on the pulse – swoon – of the era, artist and dandy Aubrey Beardsley returned from Paris, where he'd been inspired by the work of Henri de Toulouse-Lautrec, bringing with him a love for the profane and the grotesque. *The Lacedaemonian Ambassadors* is Beardsley's illustration for Aristophanes' comedy, *Lysistrata*, a highly bawdy Greek play recounting how Lysistrata sought to end the Peloponnesian War by encouraging the women of Athens to go on sex-strike. Borrowing from Shunga images he had seen in Paris, Beardsley imagines the men with huge, erect phalluses. Paired with finely curled hair and clothed in intricate regalia, traditional gender binaries are upended as Beardsley revels in the absurd and the erotic. Tragically passing away at 25, Beardsley died too young to see his legacy cemented; a trailblazer and wunderkind, he shone a light on the decadent desires of a period we'd like to pretend was much more innocent than our own.

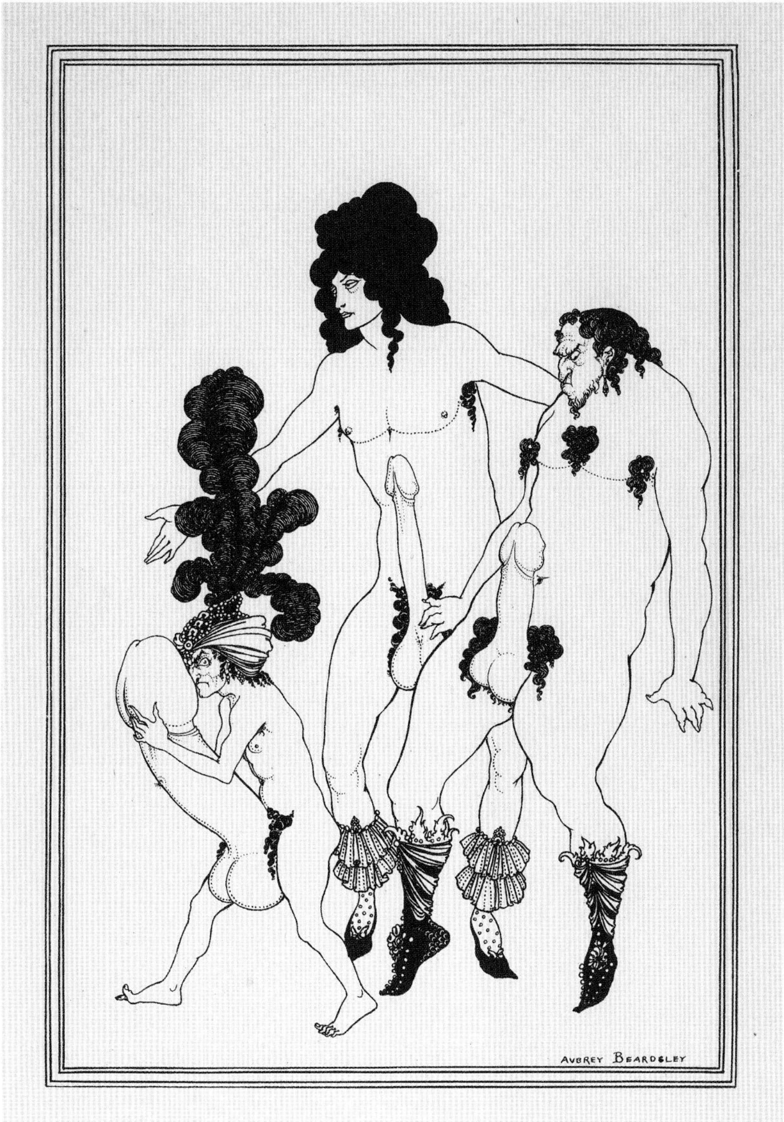

Aubrey Beardsley, *The Lacedaemonian Ambassadors*, 1896,
pen and ink over pencil on paper, 18 × 26.2 cm, The Metropolitan Museum of Art

WALTER SICKERT

La Hollandaise, c. 1906

Painting a grim reality

Erotic Art is not always a joyous celebration of passion and sensuality. Sex and danger go hand-in-hand in the artwork of Walter Sickert, who was notorious for his morbid fascination with the darker elements of erotic life. Dedicated to capturing 'real life' without the embellishments of romanticisation or beauty, Sickert used the violent and gritty locale of London's Camden Town to create a rich visual tapestry of sex, murder and disease in the early twentieth century. In *La Hollandaise*, Sickert employs his characteristically ragged, impressionistic brush strokes to portray a shabby room where a nude woman sits upright on a bed. Upending the tradition of the idealised female nude, Sickert's *Hollandaise* – perhaps a reference to the prostitute in French novelist Honoré de Balzac's work – is rendered in grubby shades of brown, green and black, her face deliberately obscured by shadow. Alarmingly, her nose appears as a gaping dark hole, which some historians have said alludes to the ravages of syphilis. This nude is then as much about fear as it is about titillation, the abject poverty of the scene turning Sickert's image into a haunting, yet sensationalist spectacle of brutality and sex.

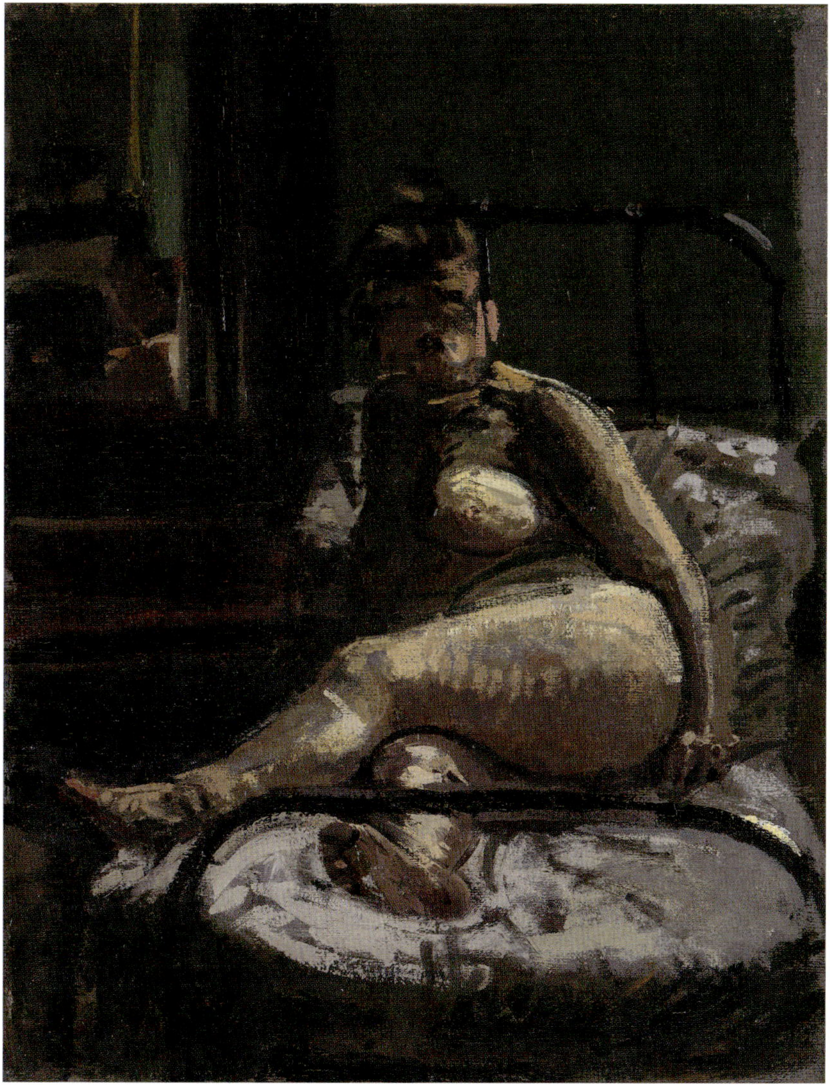

Walter Sickert, *La Hollandaise (The Dutch Girl)*, c. 1906, oil paint on canvas, 51.1 × 40.6 cm, Tate

Woman in Black Stockings, 1913

A dangerous game of dress-up

In the decadent 19th and 20th centuries, young, middle-class artists flocked to urban centres. One notable artist was Egon Schiele, and the epicentre, in his case, was Vienna. A flourishing artistic capital, Schiele was seduced by the glittering underbelly of the city and its many models and sex workers, including very young women (uncomfortably, the age of consent in Austria was then fourteen) who provided personal and artistic inspiration. *Woman in Black Stockings* depicts Schiele's muse, the seventeen-year-old Wally Neuzil. Schiele was fascinated by sex, and his many sexual works are characterised by confrontational poses and graphic, jagged lines. Here, Wally's body is contorted, her head coquettishly tilted. Looking beyond the viewer, she seems disassociated from her surroundings, the rest of the canvas white, as if situating her within a blank abyss. Dressed in flimsy fabric and thigh-high black stockings and boots, Schiele depicts Neuzil as if she is playing dress-up with her own burgeoning sexuality and desire. As controversial as Schiele is, the troubling eroticism of his work is undeniable. His figures are powerful vectors of both their own desires and Schiele's appetite, creating a sense that, as viewers, we are intruding on something primal – even obscene.

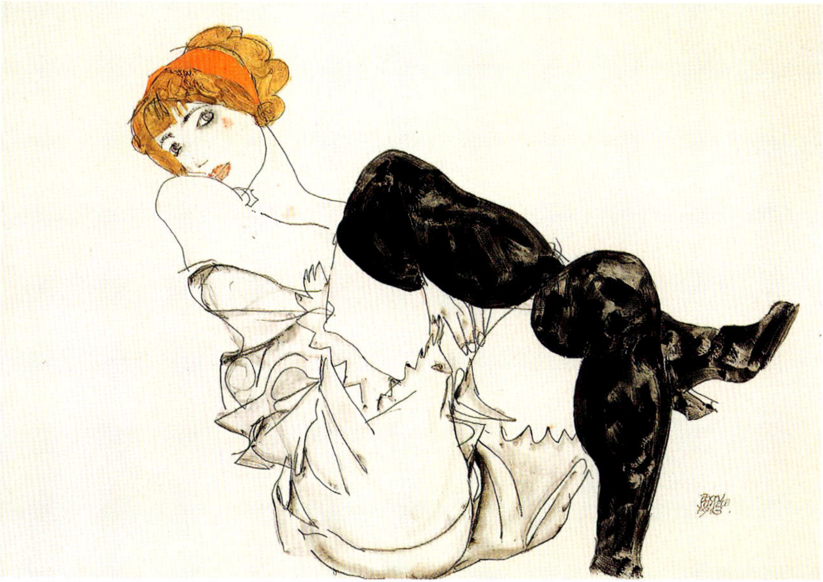

Egon Schiele, *Woman in Black Stockings*, 1913, watercolour on paper, 48 × 32.2 cm

GUSTAV KLIMT

Reclining Nude with Drapery, c. 1912–1913

Delicate outlines of erotic intensity

One of the most notable chroniclers of high society in the early 20th century, Gustav Klimt admired beautiful women as much as they admired him. His prestigious reputation enabled him to co-found the Vienna Secession, a movement made up of artists, sculptors and architects working against dreary traditionalism and instead creating an expressionistic, decorative aesthetic. In his many portraits of elite, bohemian society, he clothes women in dresses bathed in gold leaf and decks them in jewels that glitter on the canvas. In his relentless pursuit of beauty, Klimt was just as fascinated by the unadorned, private body as he was the clothed 'public'. In stark contrast to his opulent portraits, his erotic drawings strip away all artifice, depicting moments of sexual intimacy with unprecedented frankness and sensitivity. This included showing scenes of masturbation and even – god forbid – pubic hair. In this drawing of a woman pleasuring herself, her eyes are closed as if lost in reverie. It's clear that Klimt was interested in all forms of beauty, finding the erotic in manufactured visions of the elite as well as in the vulnerable, unaffected sexuality of the everyday woman.

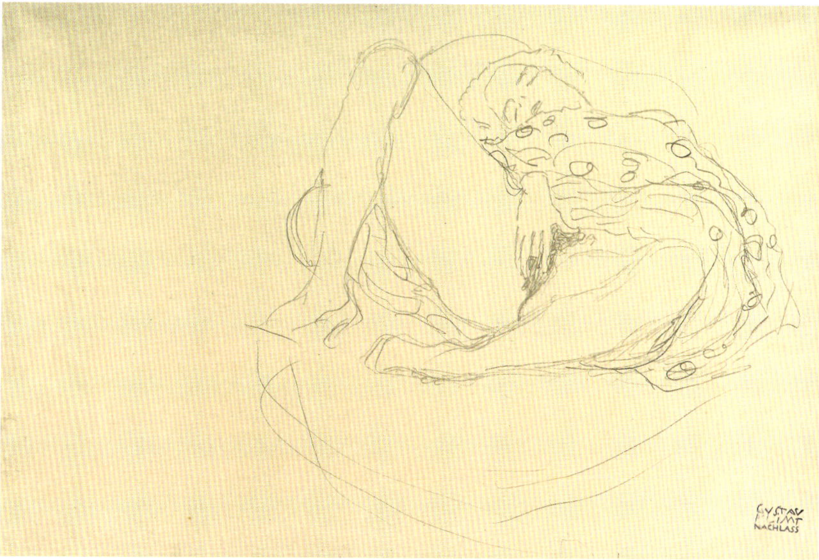

Gustav Klimt, *Reclining Nude with Drapery*, c. 1912–13, graphite,
36.8 × 55.9 cm, Metropolitan Museum of Art

JACOB EPSTEIN

Doves, 1914–15

Two birds, one stone

Many artists have flocked to Paris, but Jacob Epstein couldn't get away fast enough. While completing his sculpted winged figure for Oscar Wilde's tomb, Epstein quickly tired of the city's incessant stimulation, longing instead for a peaceful idyll on the British coast. As soon as he had finished, Epstein moved back to Sussex and began making artworks inspired by nature. Among these works were three marble sculptures of copulating doves. In this version of the sculpture, two doves are formed from the same white marble, their bodies appearing as one. A female bird, its complex form simplified into a smooth ideal, rests beneath the male. Their heads, jutting up from the block, are deliberately pared back. Realistic features are transformed into elegant curves and smooth lines to create two sensual shapes, full of erotic potential. Together, they represent the febrile sexual activity to be found throughout the natural world – but also a longing for physical intimacy.

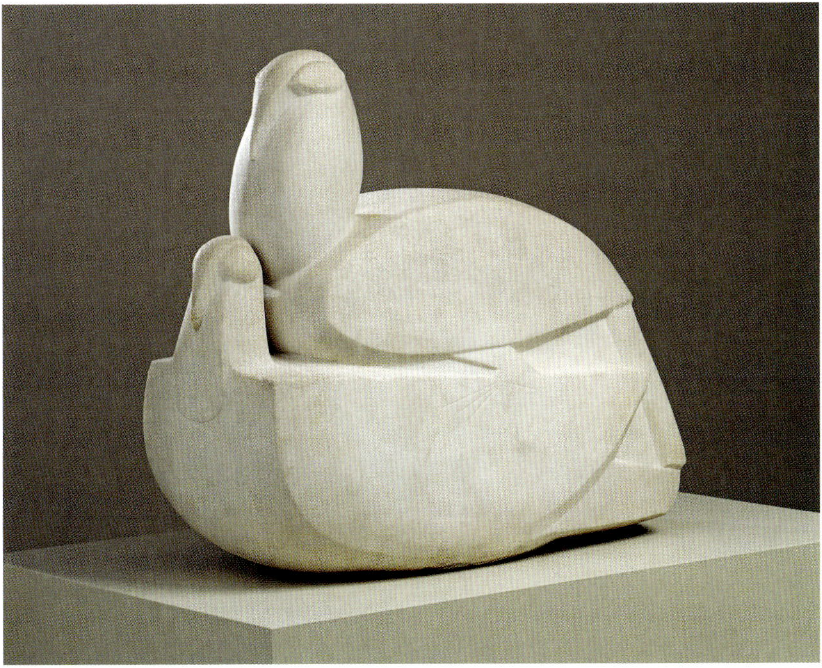

Jacob Epstein, *Doves*, 1914–15, Greek marble, 64.8 × 78.7 × 34.3 cm, Tate

MAN RAY

The Kiss, 1922

When lovers leave a trace

For the Surrealist artist Man Ray, a kiss is where it all began. In his 1922 work, Man Ray united his interest in photography with a penchant for erotic, surreal imagery. He did this by way of a photogram, a then-cutting-edge photographic technique which allowed the artist to create a photograph without a camera, laying objects atop photo-sensitive paper and exposing them to light rather than the flash of a camera. It's why *The Kiss* feels so ghostly – Man Ray and his lover, Kiki de Montparnasse, pose as the kissing couple for a fabricated image. Instead, we're left with their shadowy profiles and the traces of their touch imprinted as ghostly hands holding one another in an embrace. But across these emotional remnants, the hard black line of a darkroom tray cuts across their faces like a knife. There's something deliberately Freudian about this intervention, the omnipresence of the phallus hovering above the couple. The Surrealists were keen adopters of Freud's teachings, embracing his theories on dreams and the unconscious mind to explore the deeper layers of the human psyche. In this way, *The Kiss* is about more than just a kiss, the image charged with a sense of violent desire.

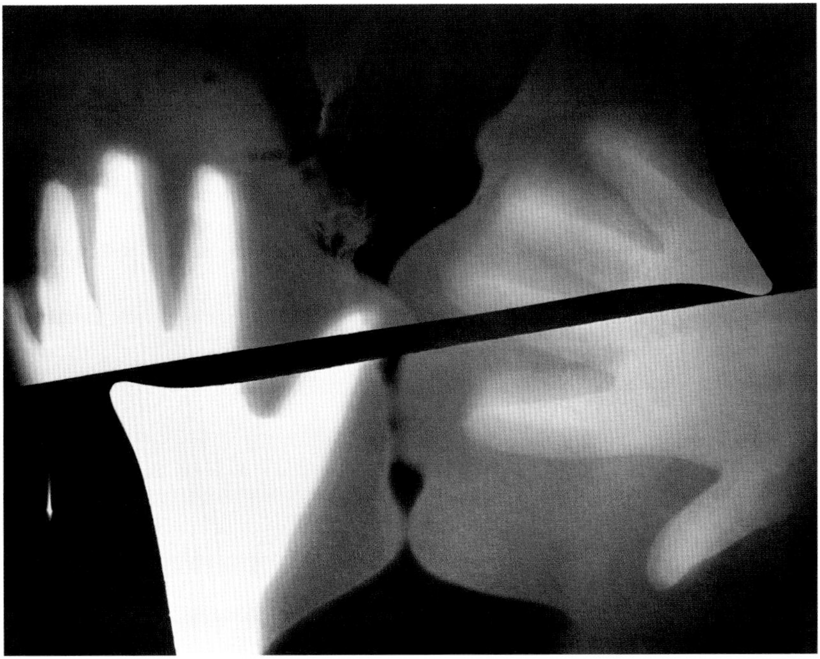

Man Ray, *The Kiss*, 1922, photogram, 23.9 × 29.9 cm, Museum of Modern Art (MoMA)

GEORGIA O'KEEFFE

Black Iris, 1926

A shocking floral arrangement

Flower or vagina? Despite rejecting the sexual inferences of her work during her lifetime, Georgia O'Keeffe has nonetheless become a poster child of erotic art. Famed for her large-scale paintings of flowers, these lustrous close-ups emphasising the dark folds of a petal or the protrusion of an erect stamen have captured erotic imaginations. In *Black Iris*, O'Keeffe took a sharp turn away from the bright, technicolour floral paintings that made her name, instead using maroons, blacks and purples to imbue her iris with a pulsating intensity. The association of the iris with new life and fertility only reinforces O'Keeffe's relationship with the erotic. Looking at O'Keeffe's *Black Iris*, it's difficult not to see the folds of a labia or the subtle definition of a clitoris. Indeed, when the work was first shown, it caused an outcry, the social historian Lewis Mumford exclaiming that O'Keeffe's exhibition was 'one long, loud blast of sex'. Yet even Mumford could admit that what matters about O'Keeffe's work is not so much what it represents, but the response it evokes in the viewer. The historian added: 'Only half the sex is on the walls; the rest is probably in me.'

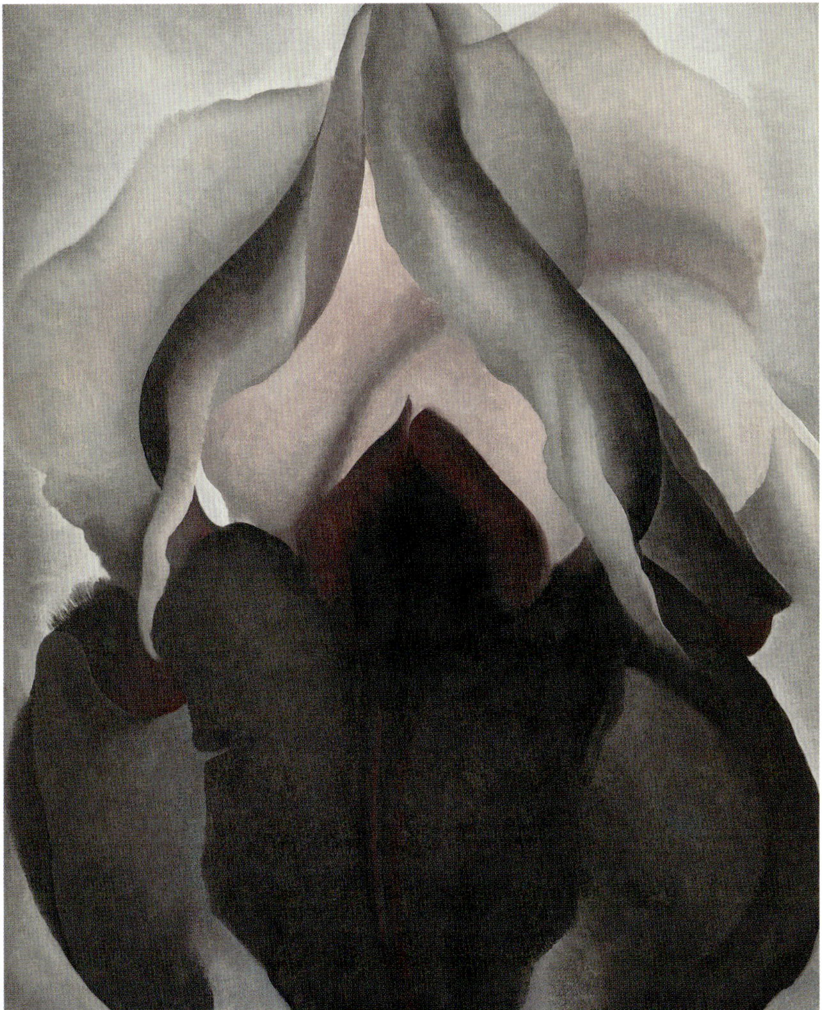

Georgia O'Keeffe, *Black Iris*, 1926, oil on canvas, 91.4 × 75.9 cm,
Alfred Stiegltiz Collection, The Metropolitan Museum of Art

DUNCAN GRANT

The Wrestlers

Fight for this love

In 2020, the Charleston Trust received a donation that was both colossal and highly unusual. The artist in question was the late Duncan Grant, and the trove was his previously clandestine life's work, with over 400 drawings, watercolours and sketches depicting luminous scenes of queer love. Following Grant's death, the collection was kept as an open secret and covertly shared among generations of friends within London's bohemian gay community. Part of the Bloomsbury Group, a coterie of writers, artists and intellectuals, Grant lived a life in vivid colour, creating an extensive collection of art, ceramics and tapestries alongside his partners, Vanessa Bell and Paul Roche. Grant's relationships were still writ large by society as taboo, and his free-wheeling, almost acrobatic depictions of lovers embracing, kissing or fondling each other were too modern, too shocking for the time. Recalling both the classical motif of nude wrestling and novelist D. H. Lawrence's infamous nude wrestling scene in his 1920 novel, *Women in Love*, Grant uses wrestling in this watercolour as a thinly veiled allusion to the passion of male intercourse, confronting masculinity and homosexuality. His figures provide a glimpse into the masquerading of desire, and how one man's passion became a rich visual testimony to a community.

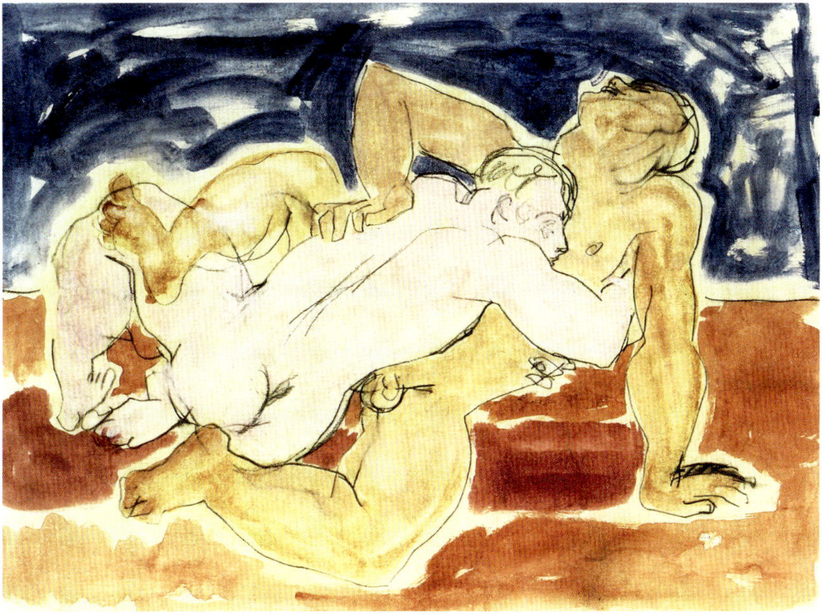

Duncan Grant, *The Wrestlers*, date unknown, watercolour

SALVADOR DALÍ

The Great Masturbator, 1929

Strange desires

In his iconic erotic work, *The Great Masturbator*, the Surrealist artist Salvador Dalí provides viewers with deep insight into his profound anxieties around sex. A meditation on shame, desire and, of course, masturbation, an abstracted face hovers above a desolate landscape, from which emerges the profile of a beautiful woman – believed to be his wife, Gala – pressed against the naked bottom half of a man. A few classic Dalí motifs are here: the restless swarm of ants festering in the folds of the misshapen face emblematise death, the looming grasshopper represents sexual anxiety, the single shadowy egg on the ground symbolises fertility. If this all sounds nightmarish, it's because it is – Dalí associated sex with paralysing dread. As a child, his father left medical textbooks around the house, their graphic illustrations of sexually transmitted diseases instilling a life-long fear of intercourse. That the artist created the work not long before his marriage is no coincidence, Dalí wrestling with fears of impotence, and the inability to sexually gratify a partner. It's no wonder then that *The Great Masturbator* is a psychoanalyst's wet dream, the work depicting the artist's conflict between his own disgust, and his strong erotic urges.

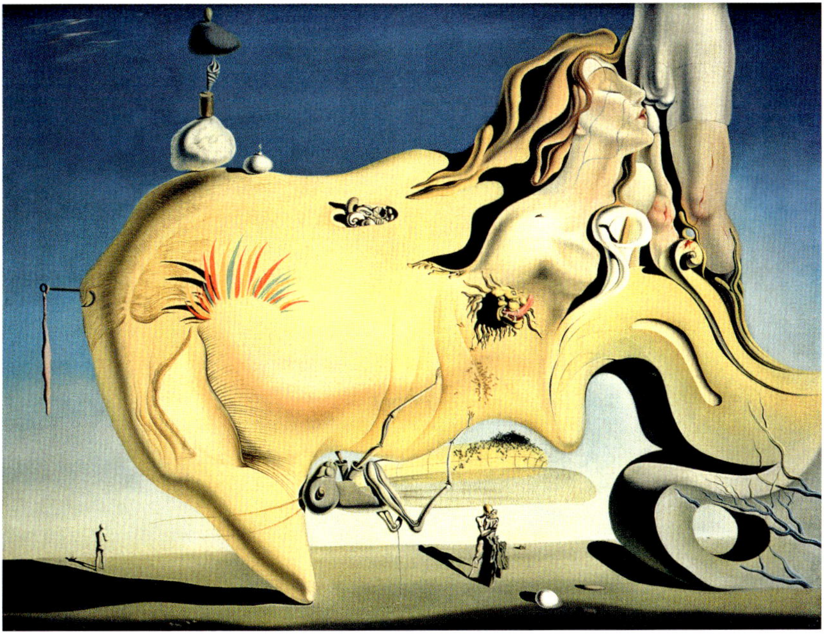

Salvador Dalí, *The Great Masturbator*, 1929, oil on canvas, 110 × 150 cm,
Museo Nacional Centro de Arte Reina Sofía (MNCARS)

HANS BELLMER

The Doll, 1936

Barbie's nightmare

That erotic art can engage with our deepest, most subconscious desires means it has the potential to confront us with what is discomfiting and disturbing. Hans Bellmer is one such challenging but visually extraordinary artist. During a time of huge emotional distress – marked by the death of his wife and his escape from Nazi Berlin – Bellmer became transfixed by the figure of the 'doll'. His biography reveals how his bizarre transfixion formed: namely, through his adolescent infatuation with his younger cousin, and happier memories of seeing *The Tales of Hoffmann*, an opera in which an animatronic doll is made into a 'real' woman. For the traumatised Bellmer, this confusing intermingling of inappropriate sexual awakening with innocent childhood nostalgia led the artist to use the doll as a site for erotic exploration, creating highly sexualised, abstracted doll-like figures, their limbs removed and broken down to their barest form. *The Doll* reveals an attempt to reject the horrors of adult life, the creation of these figures allowing the artist to return to wonder-like states of childhood while breaking down and controlling the erotic body he desires. Though the eerie adolescence of these works makes for uncomfortable viewing, they articulate the complexities of desire, where art can articulate what language cannot.

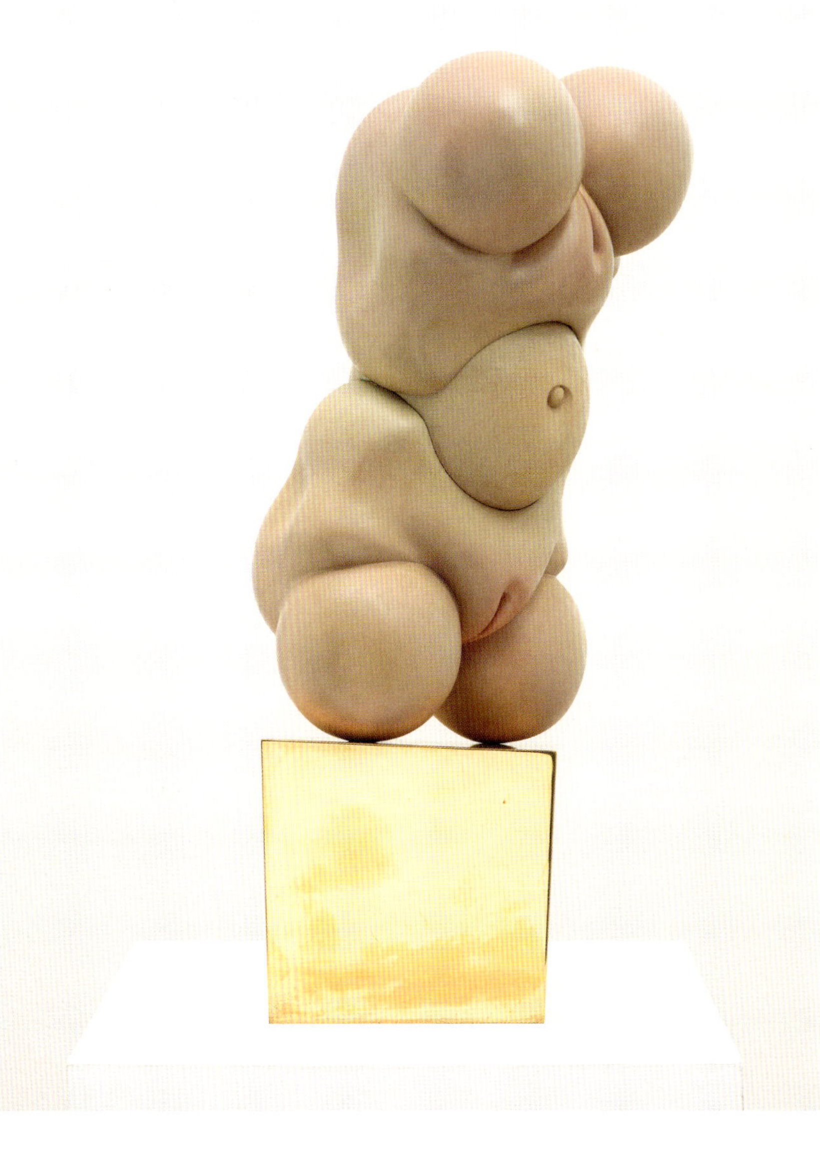

Hans Bellmer, *The Doll*, 1936, painted aluminium on brass base, 63.5 × 30.7 × 30.5 cm, Tate

ITHELL COLQUHOUN

Scylla, 1938

Under the sea

A painter, an author and a poet, British Surrealist Ithell Colquhoun dared to be different. A true firebrand, she rebelled against gender norms and revelled in androgyny, using her art to explore different modes of female sexuality, often fusing scenes from nature with bold, sexual imagery. We see this quite clearly in *Scylla*, a large oil painting where Colquhoun's interest in the natural world collides with sensuality and the body. In the image, the rock formations that make up the majority of the canvas look remarkably like thighs emerging from bath water, and the coral resting at the centre takes the form and shape of pubic hair. Named after an ancient Greek monster who survived by eating passing sailors, *Scylla* is as much a self-portrait as it is a seascape. If this is a wink and a nudge to monstrous femininity, it also engages with Colquhoun's disruptive view of gender, the legs resembling two phalluses emerging from the water. This tricksy image then becomes a vivid, daring depiction of how gender can be played with and manipulated, Colquhoun's work beautifully exploring sex beyond the status quo.

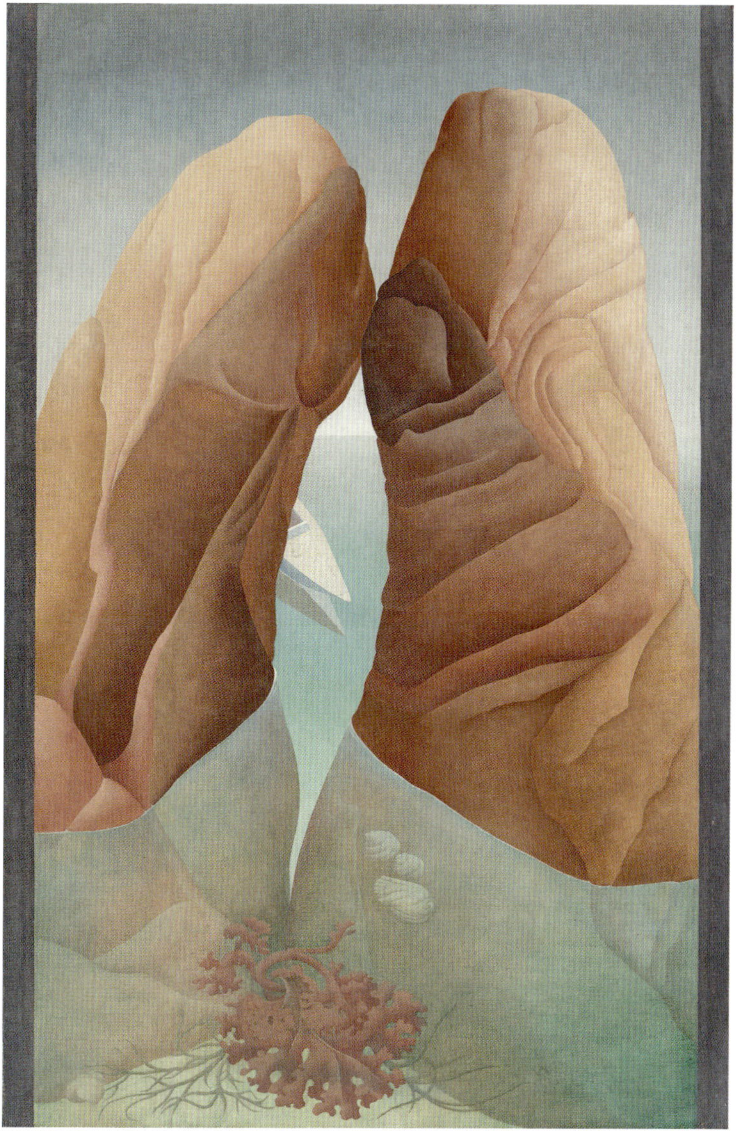

Ithell Colquhoun, *Scylla*, 1938, oil paint on board, 91.4 × 61 cm, Tate

The Shepherdess of the Sphinxes, 1941

Amazonian shepherdess nurturing feminine power

In reference to her work, Salvador Dalí once condescendingly quipped of Leonor Fini: 'Better than most, perhaps. But talent is in the balls.' In a figurative sense, Fini had balls aplenty. The avant-garde painter rejected the very notion of what a female artist should be, creating camp, hallucinatory works that often depicted women in positions of power. This sense of divine, monstrous female power is especially pronounced in her erotic work *The Shepherdess of the Sphinxes*. Situated within a desolate, dreamlike landscape – a common visualisation of the subconscious in Surrealism – an Amazonian shepherdess looks on as nubile sphinxes lounge at her feet. The sphinx was a potent symbol within Surrealist circles; writer André Breton was fixated upon the erotic potential of the sphinx, which to him encapsulated a simultaneous fear of and desire for women, while the psychoanalytical theorist Sigmund Freud aligned the sphinx with forbidden sexuality. Fini went so far as to say she wished *she* could be a sphinx, and her fascination with the feline form extended to the 23 cats living luxuriantly in her care. *The Shepherdess* celebrates the fantasy of a triumphant femininity over the landscape, nurturing an unbridled eroticism and ensuring its continuity.

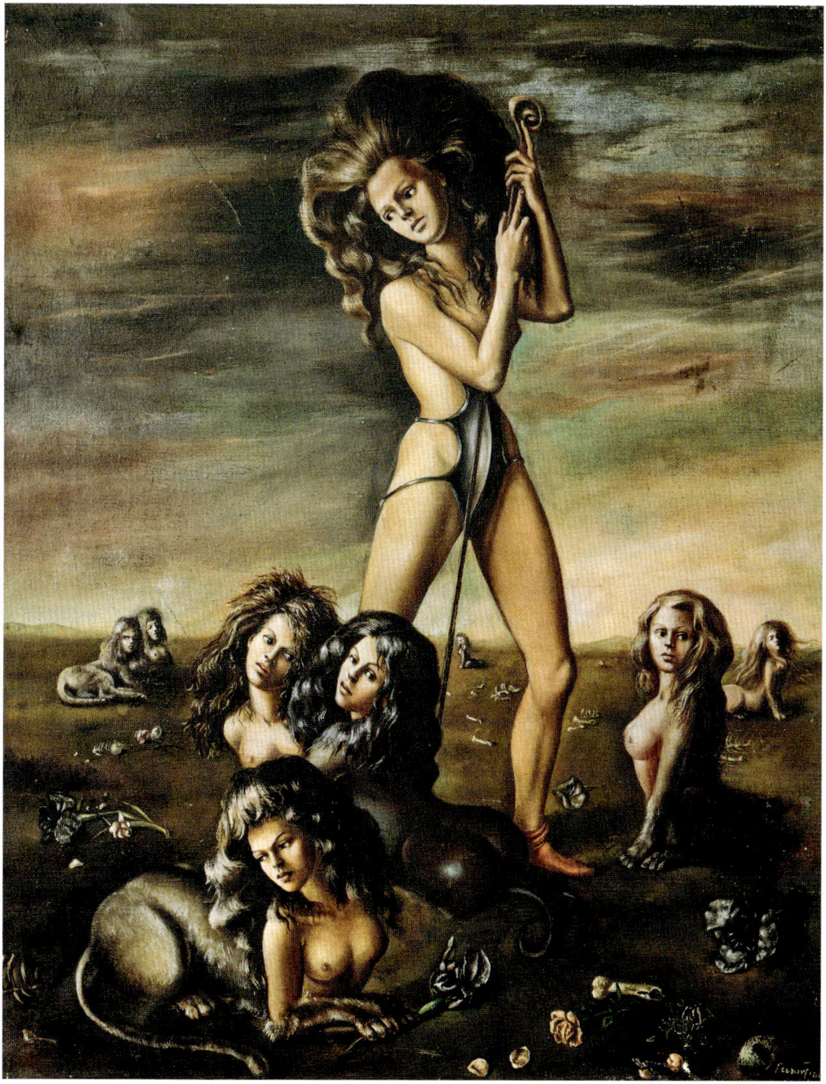

Leonor Fini, *The Shepherdess of the Sphinxes*, 1941, oil on canvas, 46.2 × 38.2 cm, Peggy Guggenheim Collection

BARBARA HEPWORTH

Wave, 1943–44

Finding the erotic in nature

Barbara Hepworth's sculptures have always been rooted in the body. Organic and sensual, the undulating curves that make up many of her works were inspired not just by the rolling Cornish landscape, but also the female form. Though some might call her more subtle than her male counterparts (Jacob Epstein's amorous marble doves (p.68) being just one example), there is a palpable erotic tension in many of her works, most notably in the abstract, curved form of *Wave*. Playing with touch and texture, Hepworth's work tempts onlookers in, each elegant curve and fine line demanding to be touched and felt. In the contrast between the warm chestnut timber and the white paint, we're reminded of pebbledash beaches and white-washed Cornish homes, but underlying the rounded form is something far more sensual. Taut bands of string cut across the sculpture, drawing the eye towards a sharp meeting point. It's a satisfying coming together of form, a biting point, a climax. In an interview, Hepworth once said, 'I draw what I feel in my body.' This approach allows her work to serve an abstracted but total expression of the self.

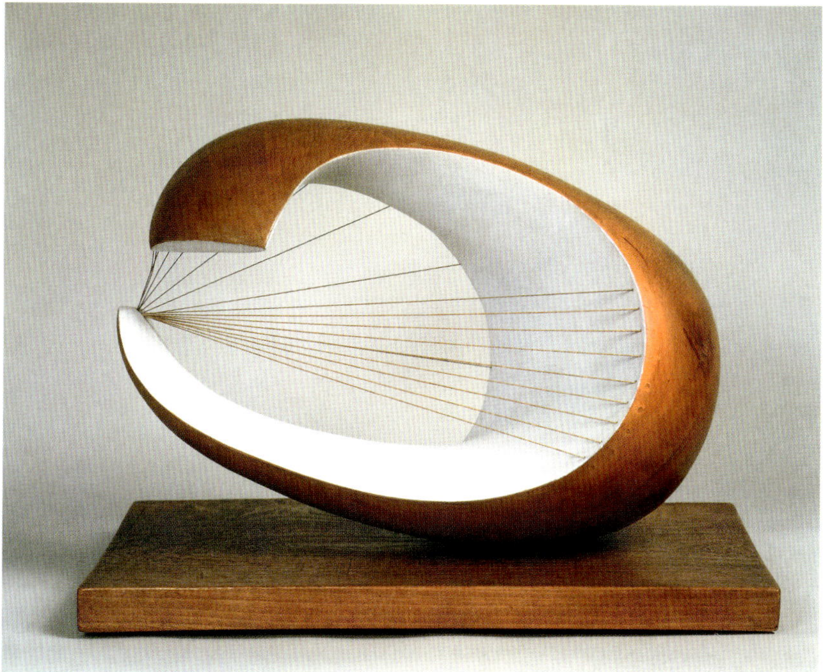

Barbara Hepworth, *Wave*, 1943–44, wood, paint and string,
30.50 × 44.50 × 21 cm, Scottish National Gallery of Modern Art

RENÉ MAGRITTE

Le Viol, 1945

Oedipal Complex à la Surréaliste

At the age of fourteen, René Magritte's life was violently, dramatically altered. In the river Sambre, not far from his family home, the schoolboy supposedly watched as his mother's drowned body was recovered from the waters, her nightgown pulled up around her face and her naked body agonisingly visible in the stream. This haunting image reverberated through Magritte's work. On one level, *Le Viol* is about how the male gaze penetrates and violates the female body, Magritte cartoonishly defiling what we imagine a woman to be by swapping out typical facial features for breasts, a naval and a pubic mound. While some scholars have suggested the painting is a wry critique of misogynistic society, it is impossible to ignore the work as a brutal outpouring of Magritte's subconscious desires; the woman's face, concealed and, at once, reassembled by the naked female body, recalls his mother's suicide. The psychoanalyst Sigmund Freud theorised that, in the early stages of their lives, all boys select their mother as their primary object of desire. We see this in *Le Viol*, where Magritte can't help but conjure the image of his mother. His memories of her follow him into his paintings, becoming entangled within his own erotic imagination.

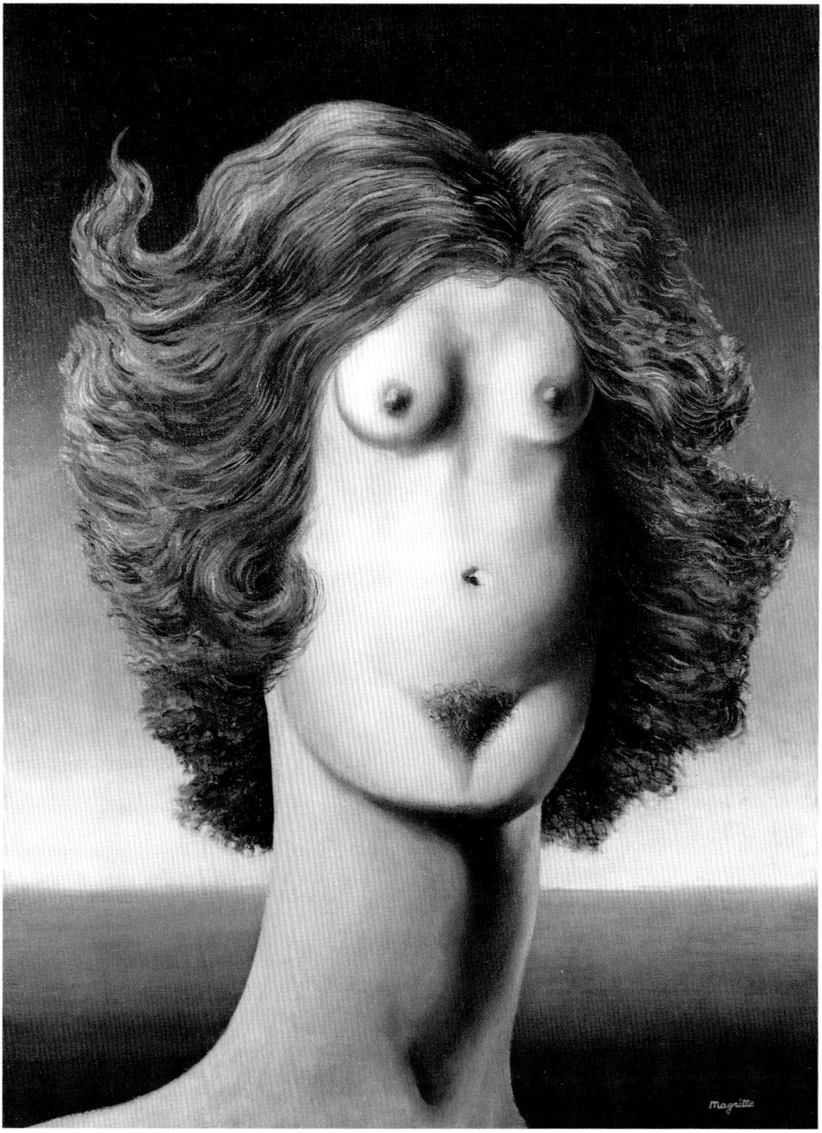

René Magritte, *Le Viol*, 1945, oil on canvas, 73.3 × 54.6 cm, The Menil Collection

JEAN DUBUFFET

Dessin érotique, 1949

Grotesque imaginings

The French artist Jean Dubuffet had a complicated relationship with art. Something of an *enfant terrible*, he dramatically 'quit' the art world several times before creating works that focused on the grotesque. After the horrors of WWII, he became fascinated by art made by non-professionals, including patients from psychiatric institutions and even the scrawls of children. (Problematically, Dubuffet and his contemporaries put non-Western artists in this category, viewing their work as 'outside' art.) In these works, Dubuffet found what he felt to be 'true' art, their lack of classical training creating something he believed more authentic and visceral, reflecting a turn towards the abstract. Seeking to emulate this freedom, he began making work he referred to as 'Art Brut'. In his erotic drawings, Dubuffet tried to evoke this sense of complete abandon – figures disgusting and enigmatic, their proportions sickening and irregular, penises moving into buttocks, hands overlapping, body parts contorting. Drawn with a continuous line on paper, Dubuffet attempts to capture the unsophisticated and debased instinctuality of sex, pairing it with a childlike, abstract style. These drawings correspond to a post-war mindset: when law and order have broken down, what is left? Only the animal can survive.

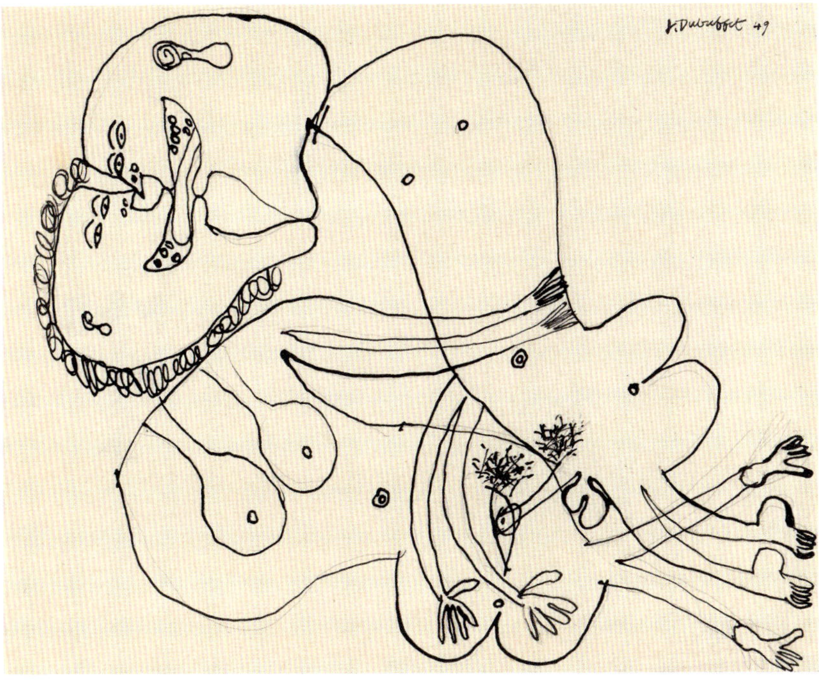

Jean Dubuffet, *Dessin érotique (Erotic Drawing)*, 1949, ink on paper, 26.7 × 21 cm, Museum of Modern Art (MoMA)

MARCEL DUCHAMP

Wedge of Chastity, 1954

A wedding gift fit for a second wife

From the artist who signed and dated his urinal, Marcel Duchamp has never been one for subtlety. Duchamp's work was underpinned by a preoccupation with how disparate things fit together, even creating a cheap pastiche of the Mona Lisa in 1919 under which he scribbled a Dalí-esque moustache and scrawled 'L.H.O.O.Q.' The crude phonetic prank, when spoken aloud in French, translates as: 'She has a hot ass.' Not just a prankster, Duchamp was a chess devotee constantly looking for hidden meanings in the everyday, fascinated by the invisible tension between objects. Typical Duchamp, then, to make erotic art from a block of wood inserted into a mass of dental gum. The flesh-like gum and organic slit – allowing the wood to slot perfectly into place – wryly encapsulate the emotional and physical mechanics of sex, and form part of a series of four small-scale 'erotic objects' exploring sex and desire. He even used the wedge as a totem of his affection, gifting it to his second wife, Alexina Matisse, the name of the work a wink to their unchaste relationship. 'We usually take it with us,' he said, 'like a wedding ring.' Two independent forms coming together as one – it's almost romantic, no?

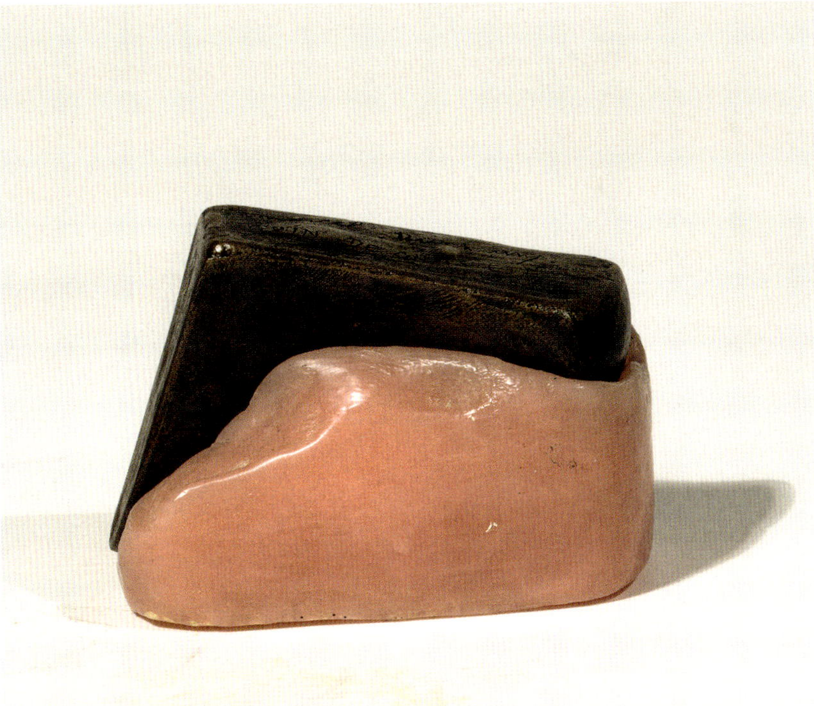

Marcel Duchamp, *Wedge of Chastity*, 1954 (cast in 1963),
bronze and plastic, 6.3 × 8.7 × 4.2 cm, Tate

CAROLEE SCHNEEMANN

Meat Joy, 1964

NSFV: Not safe for vegans

There are some video works where no single still can do them justice. Carolee Schneemann's *Meat Joy*, shown here in its 2002 recreation, is one such piece – the writhing, lively bodies frozen in the midst of febrile action. A performance captured on film, *Meat Joy* saw eight men and women engage in what Schneemann termed 'Kinetic Theatre': a type of performance where dance and movement are scored and randomised, the interplay of choreography and improvisation creating works that feel frantic and alive. Schneemann recognised how sex and the body could be used as tools from which to make art. In *Meat Joy*, she covered her body and those of the performers in raw meat, fish guts and paint, directing them to run and leap across the stage before smearing their bodies on the floor, groups of twos and threes becoming conjoined as if in a blood-soaked orgy. Though we now consider *Meat Joy* to encompass the heady eroticism lacing the 1960s – when people threw away the shackles of repression to explore newfound sexual freedom – at the time some saw the work as antithetical to the feminist cause, catering to the male gaze. In the years since, it has become a profound example of feminist eroticism: in *Meat Joy*, everyone is liberated.

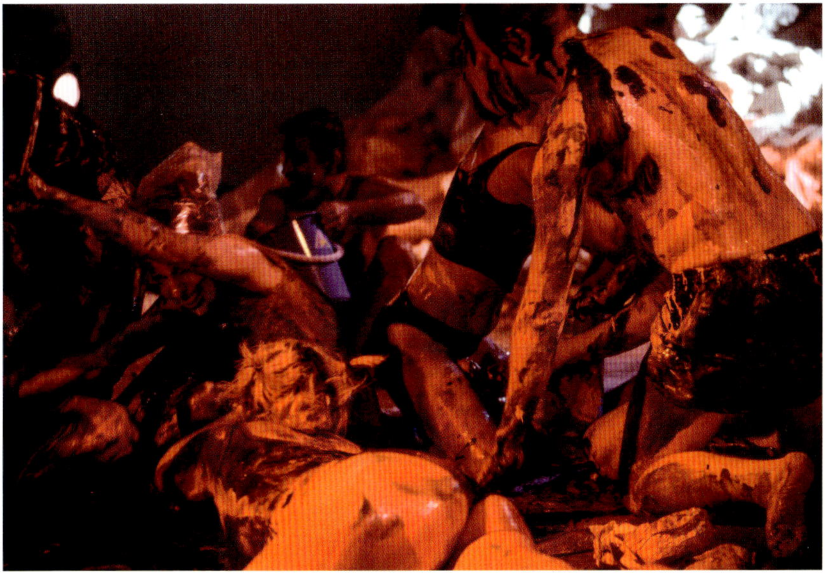

Carolee Schneeman, *Meat Joy*, 2022 recreation originally performed in 1964, shot as video in 16mm film

LEE LOZANO

No title [from Tools], 1964

A good screw

Lee Lozano has always been a hard nut to crack. A rising figure in the 1960s New York art scene, Lozano's growing contempt for the art world caused her to drop out of the scene altogether. Isolating herself from the community she had created, she also decided to boycott women, ceasing all professional and personal contact, an act that lasted until she died. This almost entirely overshadowed her career, but – like many female artists before her – Lozano has been rightfully reappraised, her conceptual works and large-scale erotic paintings offering a window into one of the most radical artists of the era. In her *Tools* series, Lozano presents ordinary objects as erotically charged instruments. Playing on several themes – perhaps most obviously the slang term 'tool' to mean penis – Lozano lampoons the sex act itself while simultaneously leaning into the inherent erotic appeal of its mechanics. By exaggerating the size of the screw and the bolt, and using a thick application of oil on canvas, Lozano graphically depicts the two objects as if in sensual, anthropomorphised motion. Deliberately confrontational, Lozano's tool paintings become a proxy for the human body – and the ways in which sex can cause us to see our bodies as objects.

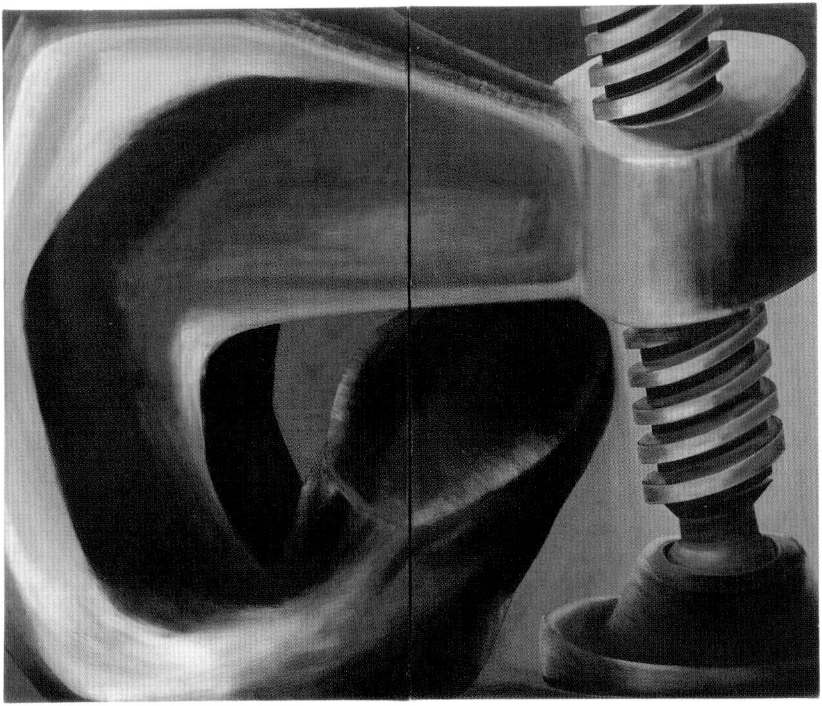

Lee Lozano, *No title [from Tools]*, 1964, oil on canvas, 2 parts, 275.2 × 336.5 × 5.2 cm, private collection

ALLEN JONES

Hatstand, Table, Chair, 1969

Objectification or emancipation?

In 1986, two unassuming women walked into the Tate gallery. Carrying bottles of paint stripper, they threw the chemical liquid onto British Pop artist Allen Jones' *Hatstand, Table, Chair*, warping the sculpture and causing significant damage. What made them do such a thing, and what can it tell us about erotic art? Created in the Swinging Sixties at a time when hemlines were growing shorter and the women's liberation movement was gaining momentum, the fibre-glass sculpture depicts three mannequin women in fetish clothing, each one occupying the position of furniture. Turning women into literal objects, it's no wonder it provoked ire from feminists, with filmmaker Laura Mulvey accusing Jones of suffering from a Freudian castration complex. Ouch. Jones argued that his work shouldn't be seen as anti-feminist, saying his aim was to create an 'iconic presence', and that chauvinistic overtones were a 'coincidental and unfortunate reading'. But it's hard to discern whether this is an avant-garde send-up of misogynistic desire or a middle finger to female empowerment. What it does reveal is submission made literal, and the power of erotic art to take otherwise unacceptable fantasies and make them tangible.

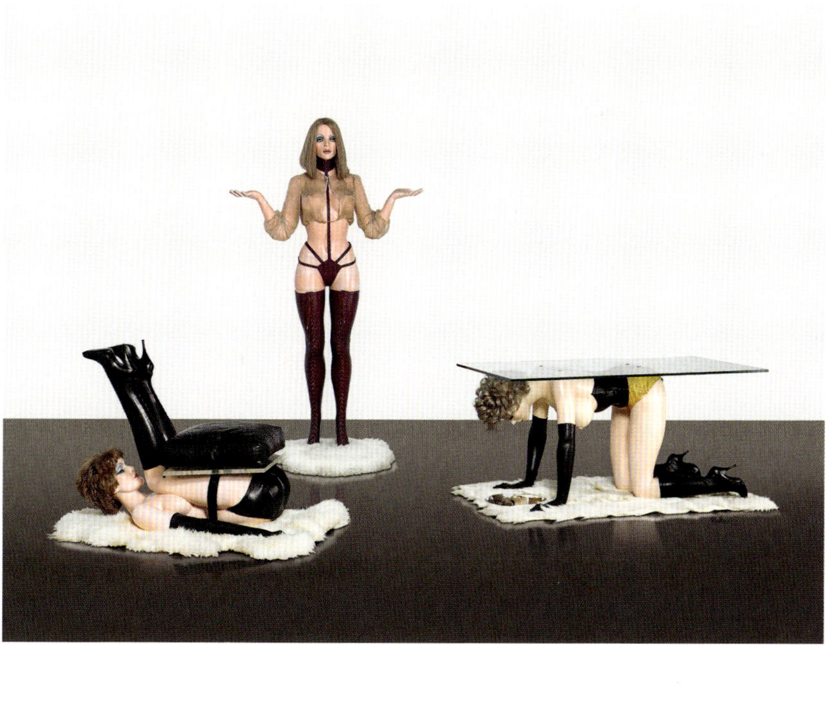

Allen Jones, *(i) Hatstand (ii) Table (iii) Chair*, 1969,
painted fibreglass, resin, mixed media, Plexiglass and tailor-made accessories,
(i) 190.5 × 107 × 33cm (ii) 61 × 130 × 76 cm (iii) 78 × 96 × 57cm, Tate

Beach Boys vol. 2, 1971

I get around

A pseudonym for the artist born as Touko Valio Laaksonen, Tom of Finland played up the pervasive kitsch imagery that filled early 20th-century magazines by creating highly eroticised images of men, rendering in pencil heavily idealised and gloriously fetishistic visions of the male body. Much of his body of work – and it is extensive, with the artist creating around 3,500 illustrations – focused on homosexual subcultures, with Tom depicting taught, muscled male labourers (an adolescent fixation of his), and later the uniformed officers he was surrounded by during his conscription in the Finnish Army. Initially creating softcore images of beefcakes as a way of bypassing US censorship laws, Tom began taking secret commissions, before the decriminalisation of male nudity meant his work could be published officially. His *Beach Boys vol. 2* presents a vision of the chiselled, all-American stud – a sculptured and glowing physique set against a beach vista, an enormous erection pushing up against his thigh. To his right, another strong-jawed man in leatherwear opens his mouth expectantly. It's fun in the sun and speaks to Tom of Finland's radical celebration of homosexuality.

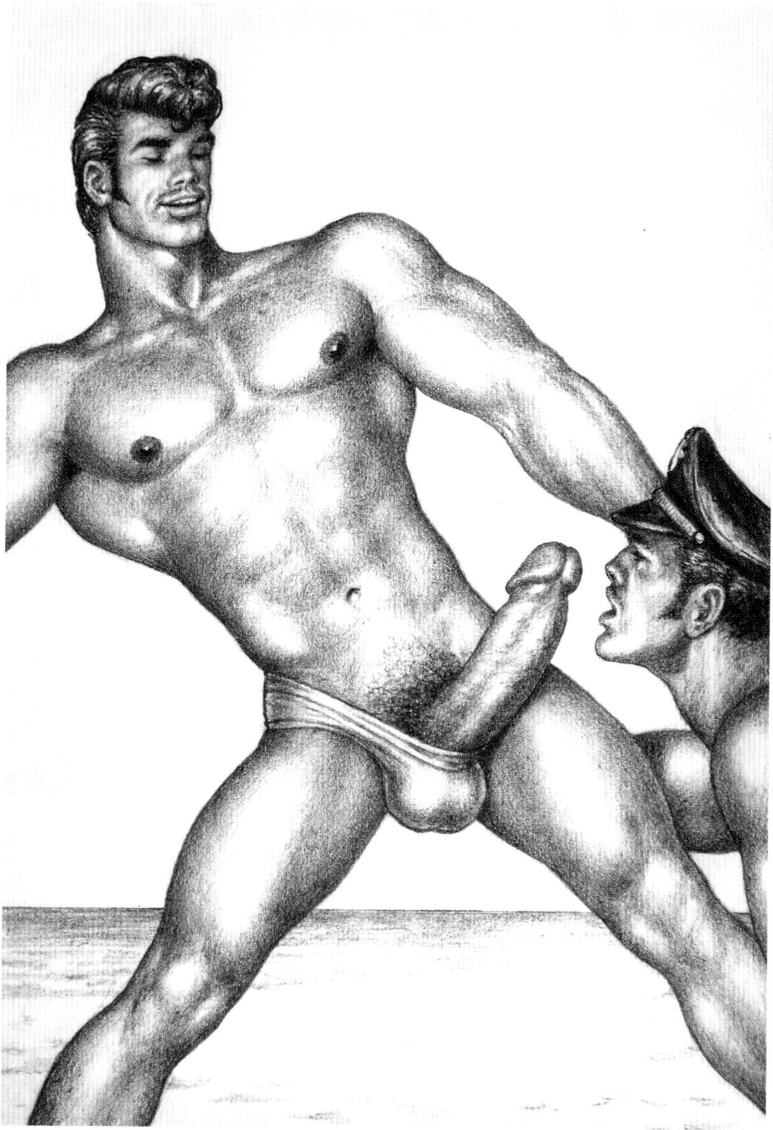

Tom of Finland, *Beach Boys vol. 2*, 1971, graphite on paper, 24.8 × 17.8 cm

JOAN SEMMEL

Erotic Yellow, 1973

Technicolour sexscapades

In 1970, Joan Semmel returned to her hometown of New York from Spain disillusioned. Instead of the simmering sexual revolution she had hoped to find in Europe, she was faced with 'sexual commercialisation'. Determined to challenge this, Semmel set out on a mission to create art that redefined sexual liberation on her own terms. Her response was a series called *Sex Paintings*. Semmel was looking to create artworks of parity: she believed that the nexus of female oppression could be found in the bedroom, and made large-scale works depicting graphic, explosive scenes of sexual expression. Semmel's curious choice of colour – her nude figures painted in hues of crimson, candy-floss pink, green or buttercup yellow – is emblematic of this large-than-life expression, sexual encounters attesting to liberatory erotic possibilities. In *Erotic Yellow*, a female figure grasps the groin of her male lover, the two figures interlocked. Keen to depict the revolutionary sex she'd anticipated in Spain, these were paintings taken from life, Semmel arranging sessions with models who, with consent, would have sex while Semmel took photographs. It's this combination of real sexual life, alongside Semmel's surreal, ultra-fantastic colour, that turns these vibrant works into something revolutionary, pleasure transcending race and identity to become a projection of radical possibility.

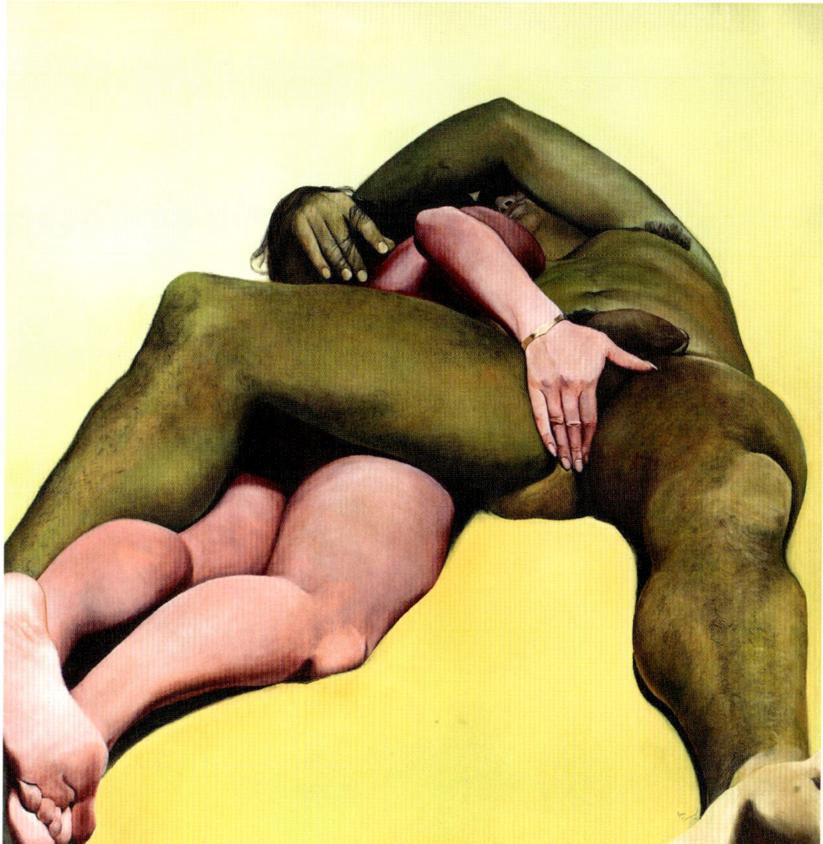

Joan Semmel, *Erotic Yellow*, 1973, oil on canvas, 182.9 × 182.9 cm

FRANCIS BACON

Two Figures with a Monkey, 1973

The animal that lurks within

The line between man and beast has always been contested in the work of Francis Bacon. Fascinated by animals from an early age – helped in part by his father's career as a racehorse trainer – as an adult, Francis Bacon purportedly claimed to find the smell of horse dung 'sexually alluring', indicating a powerful, if disturbing, erotic connection between the artist and the animal world. That Bacon was also allergic to most animals, with contact triggering his chronic asthma, only heightened his morbid attraction. More than just containing animals, Bacon's work speaks to the animal within, his frightening, nightmarish visions of intimacy reducing his male muses to their most primal state. In *Two Figures with a Monkey*, two abstracted bodies morph violently into one upon an elevated bed. Bacon's characteristic swooping brushstrokes add to a sense of aggressive movement; colour and form collide as the figures penetrate one another. With chaos ensuing above, a monkey swings ominously in the foreground. The unrepressed animalism of the monkey – our closest non-human relative – acts as a metaphor for the id: a psychoanalytic term for the part of the unconscious that works to satisfy instinctual desires. Here, Bacon suggests: perhaps we're not so different after all?

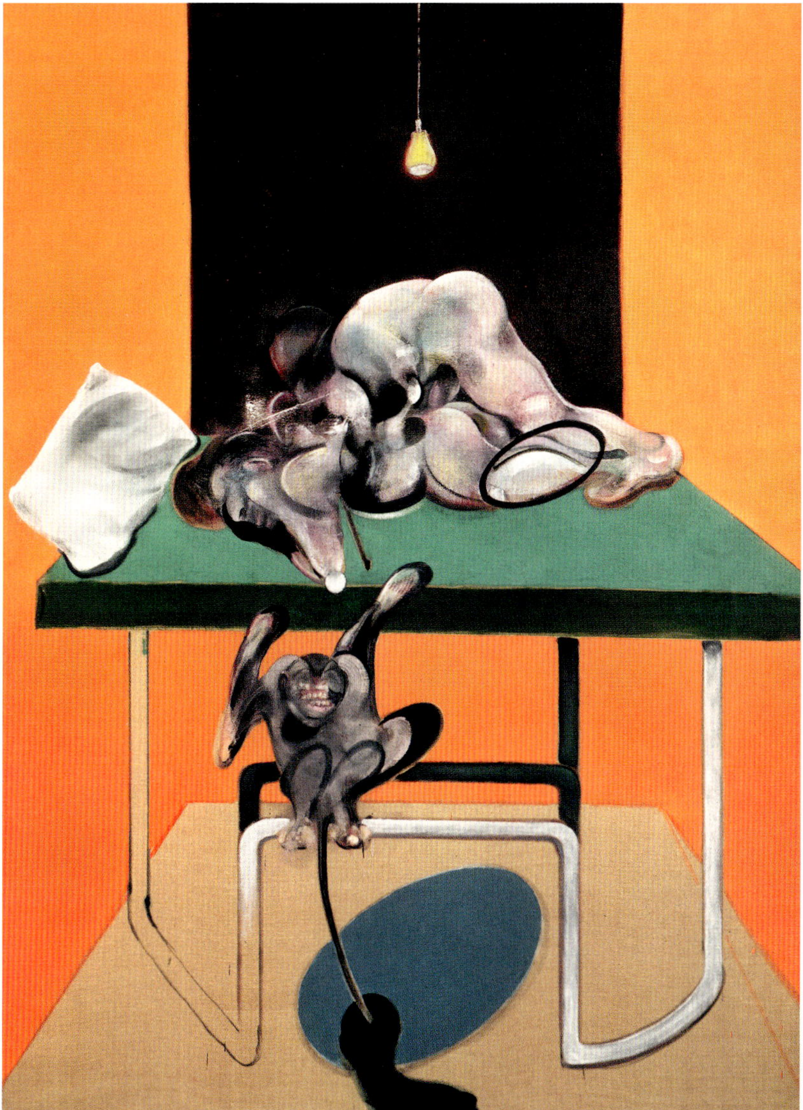

Francis Bacon, *Two Figures with a Monkey*, 1973, oil on canvas, 198 × 147.5 cm

LYNDA BENGLIS

Artforum Advertisement, 1974

Mad Men

You can imagine the shocked expressions of artists, curators and art-world wannabes as they opened their copies of the November 1974 edition of *Artforum* to discover a nude, two-page advertisement of Lynda Benglis sporting a rather large sex toy. Dressed in nothing but a pair of sunglasses, Benglis poses rigidly, her body taut, glistening and complete with aggressive tan lines. Promoting her upcoming exhibition by means of a series of 'sexual mockeries', Benglis shot a number of ads as an extension of the art itself. Repelling the conventional male gaze, her *Artforum* image takes the societally approved attractive female body and unseats it, her hip cocked in a semi-squat, topped off with an enormous, veined, double-ended dildo. Though it has since achieved cult status, Benglis's advert divided opinion quite radically at the time. Some felt that Benglis was simply cashing in – ironic considering the work set out to mock how unashamedly artists 'sell out' – while many more worried the work was a backwards step for feminist art. For Benglis, the ad captures the erotic potential of parody, ridiculing gendered expectation and role-play, the artist simultaneously playing the role of pin-up and playboy, and ultimately becoming 'a statement of freedom [...] a revelation of unashamedly expressing myself.'

Lynda Benglis, *Artforum Advertisement*, 1974, *Artforum* vol. 13, no 3, magazine, 26.7 × 26.7 cm

JUDY CHICAGO

Female Rejection Drawing, 1974

Mind the teeth!

It was the 1960s in sleazy, swinging New York City, and Judy Cohen was feeling blue. Desperate to be taken seriously by the art world, Judy was 'trying to act, and make art, as if I were a man.' This all changed in the 1970s. As the women's liberation movement tore through the country, ripping through the collective mindset of America's housewives, Judy Cohen rejected her surname and switched it to 'Chicago'. The radical change in the air inspired Chicago to make work that celebrated, rather than exorcised, her gender, writing about and shaping a practice that centred on a new kind of art history: the history of women's art. This focus on gender is explicit in *Female Rejection Drawing*, where Chicago uses vibrant, technicolour pencils to depict vaginal iconography. The form emerges from the centre like an exotic fruit, with layers peeling back into sharp, teeth-like petals. In cursive handwriting beneath, Chicago explains her motivations: taking the erotic symbol of the vagina and turning it away from the male gaze. The imagery evokes the concept of 'vagina dentata', symbolising emasculation, or castration. But in these shimmering, iridescent colours, Chicago celebrates the vagina as a life-giving force at the centre of creativity. If that scares men, so be it.

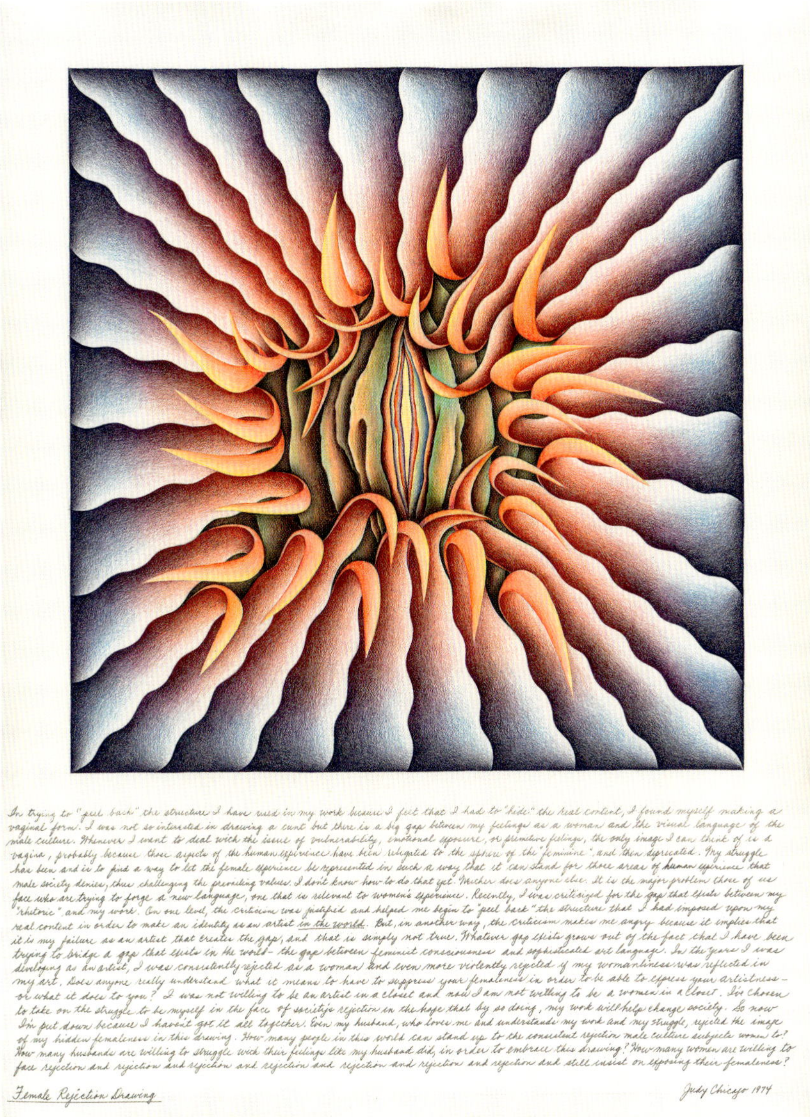

Judy Chicago, *Female Rejection Drawing*, 1974, coloured pencil and graphite on paper, 101.6 × 76.2 cm, San Francisco Museum of Modern Art (SFMOMA)

MARINA ABRAMOVIĆ

Rest Energy, 1980

Holding their lives in their hands

The art world is punctuated by partnerships that transcend the boundaries of convention, but few are as iconic as that of Abramović and Ulay. Their union was anything but ordinary, marked by an intensity mirrored in their art. Meeting in Amsterdam in 1976 against a backdrop of fervent political change across Europe, the pair began creating powerful work that evoked the unspoken dynamics of romantic and sexual relationships with performances that were often physically demanding, dangerous and disturbing. Their 1976 performance *Relation in Space* saw the naked lovers run full pelt at one another, bodies painfully colliding, while in *Breathing Out, Breathing In* (1977), the pair locked mouths for 19 minutes, using one another for oxygen while their nostrils were blocked with cigarette filters. After a 12-year partnership, they eventually chose to separate by each walking the length of the Great Wall of China, meeting in the middle to say their final goodbye. Their most threatening, and most erotic work, is *Rest Energy*. This white-knuckle performance demanded perfect, harmonious opposition; even the slightest misstep could have resulted in the death of Abramović. There's something erotically compelling about the work, as Ulay and Abramović demonstrate the close relationship between love, sex and self-annihilation. Just don't try this at home.

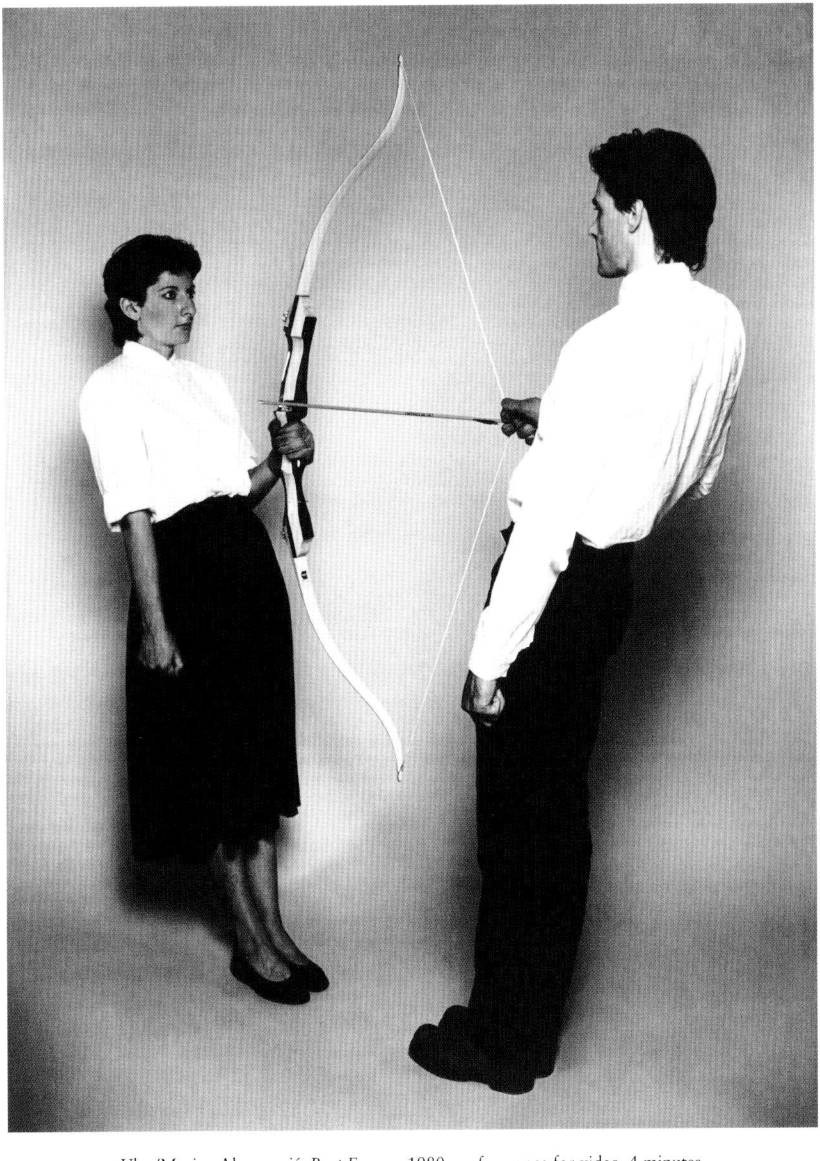

Ulay/Marina Abramović, *Rest Energy*, 1980, performance for video, 4 minutes, ROSC' 80, Dublin, courtsesy of the Marina Abramović Archives

DAIDŌ MORIYAMA

Tights in Shimotakaido, 1987

Fishnet fantasies

In 1986, Daidō Moriyama went to a cafe with his girlfriend. While drinking a cup of coffee, he glanced at her legs, becoming entranced by her fishnet tights. Taking out his camera, the photographer shot two rolls of film in little over an hour, a collection that was to form part of a photo series dedicated to the latent eroticism emerging from the images. In close-up, Moriyama's *Tights* are abstracted works, the circular and hexagonal criss-crosses looking somewhere between the interior chambers of a beehive and Stanley Kubrick's meticulously designed sets. What is evoked is highly sensory: the tension of material pulled across skin, the feeling of flesh bound and wrapped tight. Elegant lines reveal shapely calves, or the gentle, undulating curve of an inner thigh, the legs becoming sculptural rather than figurative. Moriyama was fascinated by the seedy nature of urban life in post-war Japan, where you could lose yourself in the sprawl of the city. That the models in the *Tights* series are anonymous figures, divorced from a face or a name, only adds to this sense of erotic alienation, with Moriyama playing to the generational complexes of an era.

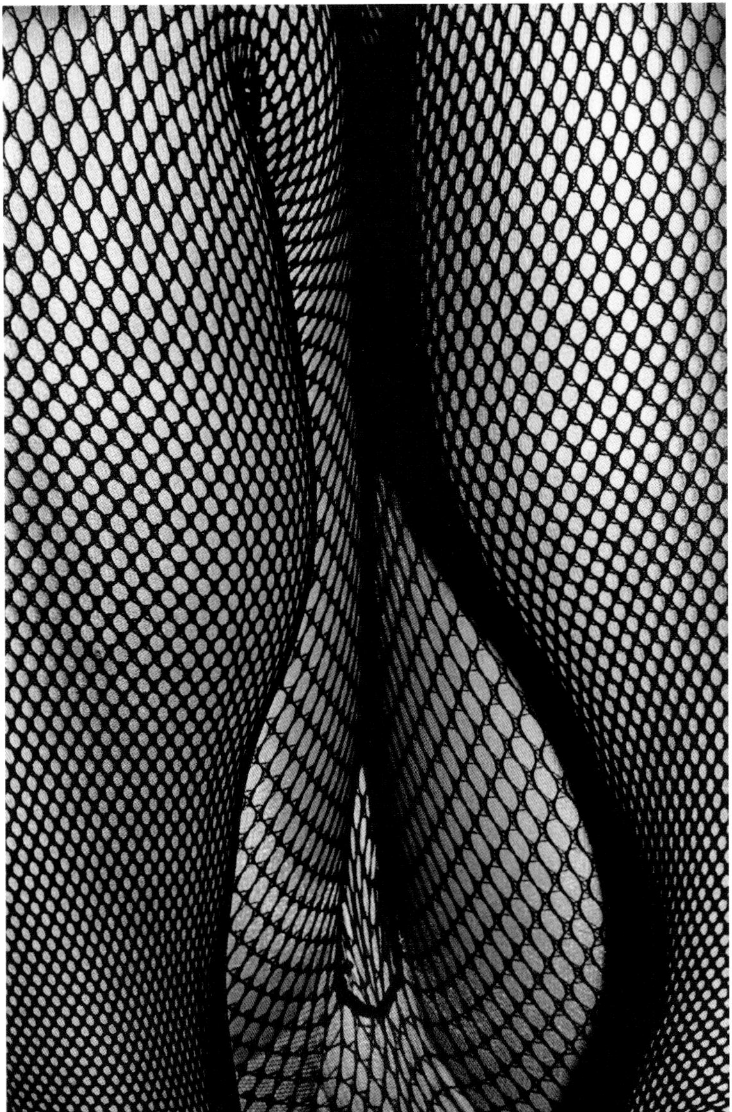

How to create a beautiful picture 6: Tights in Shimotakaido,
Daidō Moriyama, 1987, silver gelatin print, 46 × 56 cm

SARAH LUCAS

Au Naturel, 1994

Sexuality stripped down

Part of the ragtag gang of artists known as the YBAs (Young British Artists), Sarah Lucas's work often fuses sardonic – even slapstick – humour with profoundly political meditations on bodily autonomy. Translated from French as 'in the nude', Lucas plays with classical connotations of the naked body and, in her sculpture-cum-installation, subverts them. Lucas knocks back idealised depictions of nudity down to their barest, and most stupid, form. On the floor lies a shabby mattress, two oranges and a stiff 'erect' cucumber taking the position of the 'man', while two melons crudely stitched into the fabric and a dented metal bucket become the 'woman'. It's a biting and deliberately provocative take on gender, and the reductive ways in which art commodifies and displays relationships. But it's not all wry laughs and eye-rolling. There's a tangible warmth to Lucas's work, this cutting down of sexual function a celebration of the silliness inherent in sexual exchange. Breasts that look like melons, ball sacks that look like oranges; we've all been there. Here, Lucas advocates for a more humane, less worshipful take on sex and relationships, her work laughing us all into bed.

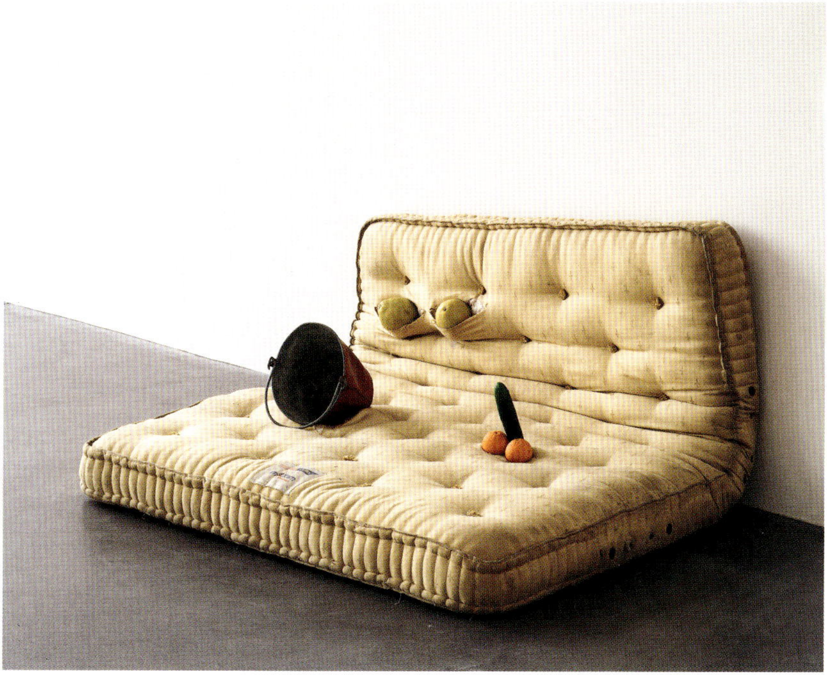

Sarah Lucas, *Au Naturel*, 1994, mattress, water bucket, melons, oranges and cucumber, 84 × 168 × 145 cm

TRACEY EMIN

Everyone I Have Ever Slept With 1963–1995, 1995

A body count that disrupted art history

A renegade darling of the YBA movement, Emin has been a noted provocateur since the early 1990s. Though her drawings of masturbation are more explicitly sexual, *Everyone I Have Ever Slept With* sees Emin wrestling with her own vulnerability, allowing viewers a glimpse into the artist's erotic life. Inside a flimsy tent are stitched the names of every person Emin has ever shared a bed with, revealing an intimate patchwork interior charged with memory. The woven roster includes ex-boyfriends, friends and her own grandmother, with Emin slyly including platonic relationships, leading one reviewer to exclaim: 'She's slept with everyone – even the curator!' But there's sincerity here, too. Inside the work, two numbered foetuses interlink the sexual with the biological, combining to make Emin's tent a cathedral in miniature: a shrine to her loves and losses. Its legacy is potent: Emin refused to sell the piece to collector Charles Saatchi, given his collaboration with Margaret Thatcher. Years later, the work met its untimely demise in a blazing warehouse fire. Yet Emin does more than deliver cheap shock. Instead, this confessional self-portrait in tarpaulin shows how the erotic can shape a life.

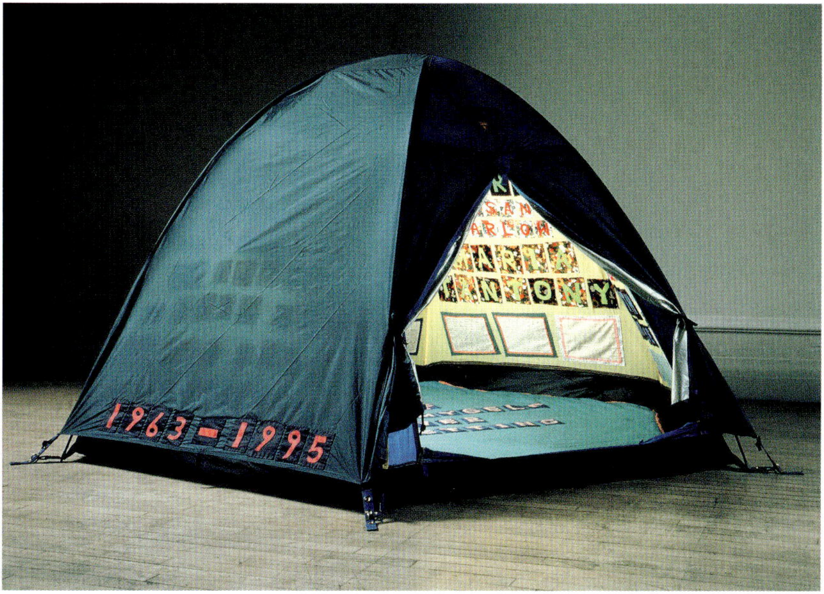

Tracey Emin, *Everyone I Have Ever Slept With 1963–1995*, 1995,
appliquéd tent, mattress and light, 122 × 245 × 215 cm

MARLENE DUMAS

Fingers, 1999

Dumas' finger-up to shame

Throughout her career, Marlene Dumas has used her work to challenge taboos. Reflecting on her upbringing in Apartheid-era South Africa, Dumas contemplated the meaning of 'truth' amid censorship, and the struggle between shame and free expression. This is keenly felt in her erotic works, which aggressively centre women's bodies and their pleasures. Borrowing from Expressionism's aesthetic style, Dumas' work seeks to dispel romantic notions of the nude, sexual body, and instead evoke carnal realities. In *Fingers*, we see Dumas' characteristically bold brushstrokes suggest a woman using her fingers to masturbate, her face hidden from view. Inspired by the newly uncensored porn that emerged in the 1970s, Dumas wanted to study how we perform our private and public lives, ripping up the dividing line between the two and painting her subject in a pose proudly unabashed; her figure's turned back and splayed fingers a daring provocation aligned with the pursuit of freedom. Dumas challenges us to question why we find depictions of sex – more importantly, female pleasure – so shocking.

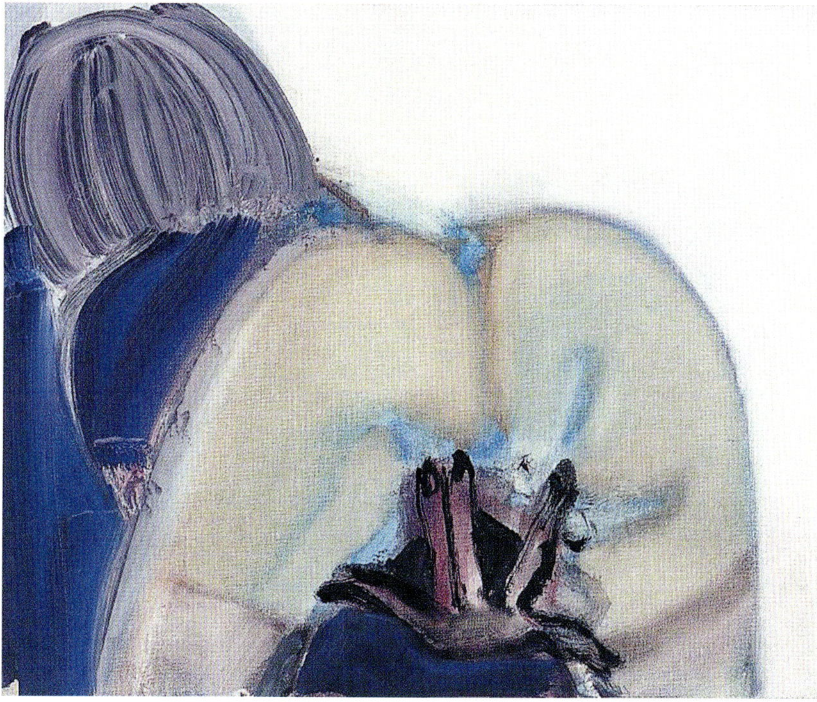

Marlene Dumas, *Fingers*, 1999, oil on canvas, 40 × 50 cm

CATHERINE OPIE

Untitled (from the O Portfolio), 1999

A butch fantasy

Beginning as a response to Robert Mapplethorpe's *X Portfolio* collection (specifically an S&M-styled self-portrait of the artist penetrating himself with a whip), photographer Catherine Opie wanted to centre the lesbian experience, swapping bull-whips and assholes for tender yet electric depictions of female love, desire and kink. In this image, we see the clasped hands of an unnamed figure, wrists bound in leather cuffs linked by chain, fingers tenderly interlaced. Forgoing Mapplethorpe's thrilling muscular sexual gratuity, the other works in Opie's series feature granular close-ups of bondage rope against a black background, hanging chains, a thigh in suspenders and the face of a woman closing her eyes as she caresses her partner's throat. Dramatically magnified, the body is utterly dematerialised, any narrative thread obscured from full view. The effect is hazy and dreamlike, as if fragments of a memory are being pieced together; the images belong to no one woman and so, by extension, belong to all women. Opie ultimately departs the secretive, clandestine world of S&M, and seeks instead to invite, turning the images into a universal erotic story.

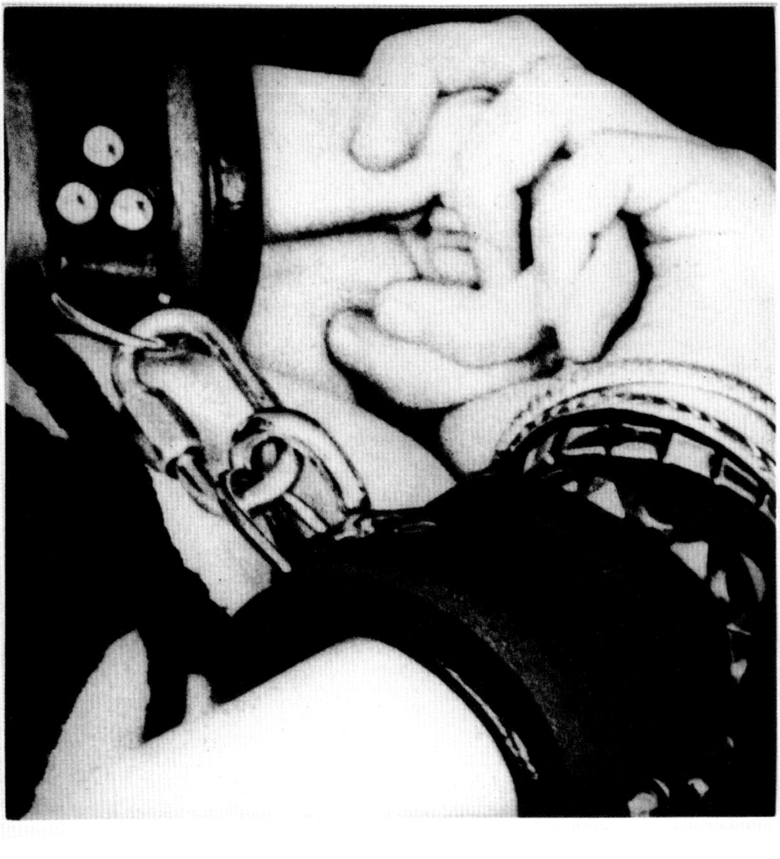

Catherine Opie, *Untitled (from the O Portfolio)*, 1999,
7 photogravures in O black embossed box, order in portfolio: #3, 46.99 × 35.56 cm

WOLFGANG TILLMANS

The Cock (kiss), 2002

An iconic kiss

Initially known for capturing the intimate lives of ordinary people in club basements, apartment bathrooms and out in nature, Wolfgang Tillmans is today recognised as one of the most defining visual storytellers of his generation, his work as relatable as it is profound. However, one image in particular has a lingering effect. In *The Cock (kiss)*, Tillmans brings to life the hedonism of young, queer culture by training his lens on a passionate kiss between two men, their faces pressed into one another, pink lips, flushed ears and sweaty hair dominating the image. As nostalgic as it is erotic, *The Cock (kiss)* evokes the pulsating heat on a club dancefloor, where people can connect in the darkest of corners, their private moment spotlit by the sudden glare of Tillmans' camera flash. This close-up deepens one sweaty club kiss into a heartfelt, intimate evocation of desire. It's visceral – you can practically taste the sweat-streaked skin, feel the rough graze of stubble against your cheek. The image has also become a rallying cry, taken to protests and used as a defiant finger-up to homophobia after having been vandalised while being exhibited in the US. As such, the photograph's enduring power goes beyond capturing a fleeting moment between two people: it's a lasting symbol of hope and freedom.

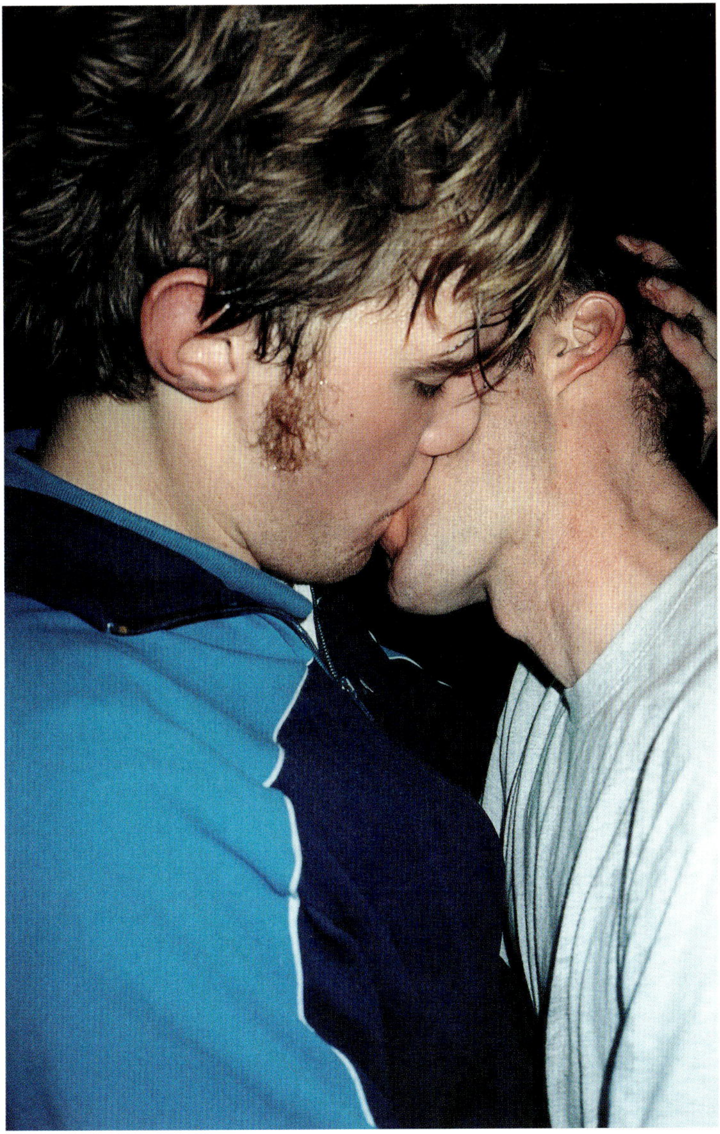

Wolfgang Tillmans, *The Cock (kiss)*, 2002

RON ATHEY

Self-Obliteration, 2007

The body keeps the score

When people talk about performance artist Ron Athey, they might first recall the time he pulled strings of gleaming white pearls from his anus, or when he inserted a baseball bat inside his rectum. They might also reference *Self-Obliteration*, which starts with Athey brushing a pristine blonde wig and ends with his blood-smeared body writhing atop a sheet of glass. Amid the shock, mutilation and gore, Athey turns his own body into an erotic object, as sculptural as any marble, martyred saint. Ending his performance with the stillness of an entombed pharaoh, Athey's body becomes a site of death, redemption and resurrection. This is mirrored by the audience members who, in accordance with the participatory nature of his performances, often physically comfort Athey as he endures. Athey is HIV-positive and, creating his work in the aftermath of the AIDS crisis, responds to his personal experience of witnessing community caregiving. In this he draws links to Christian martyrdom, expressing his own trauma and survivor's guilt through performance. As difficult as Athey's work is, it's this conflict between pain, pleasure, care and destruction that makes works like *Self-Obliteration* so compelling. You might wince, but you shouldn't look away.

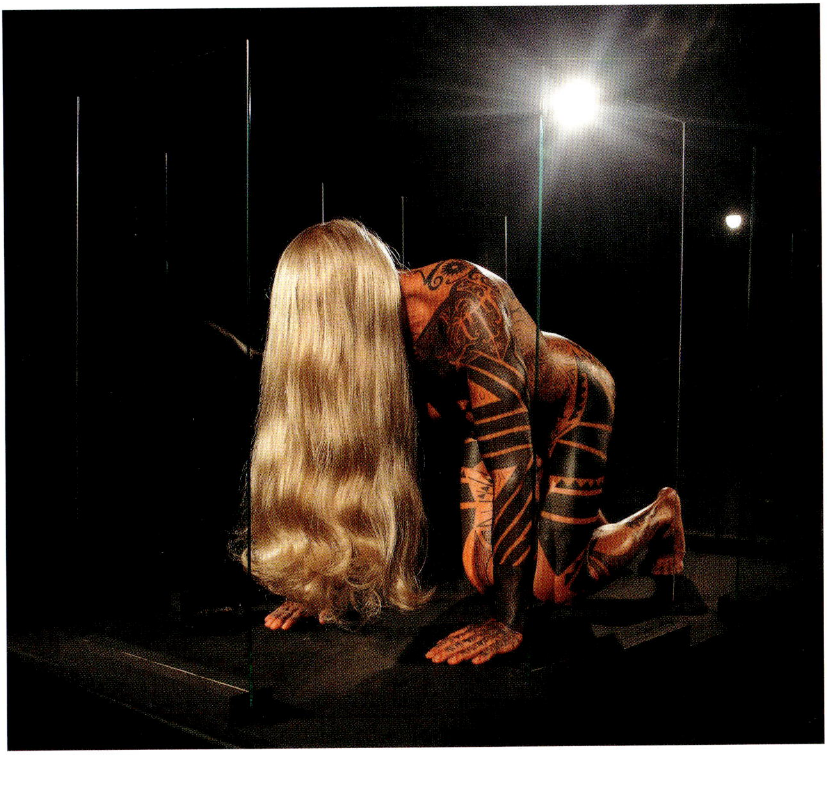

Ron Athey, *Self Obliteration*, 2007, performance, 30 minutes

PAUL CHAN

Sade for Sade's Sake, 2009

A very dirty projector

As a man born of high rank and nobility, few expected the young Marquis de Sade to become a writer infamous for his indecent, profane and psychologically disturbing novels – or to live out his final years incarcerated in an asylum. Yet despite his dismal end, the memory of de Sade lives on and has – rightly or wrongly – inspired the likes of the Surrealists, Sigmund Freud and the contemporary artist Paul Chan. In the nearly six-hour video installation *Sade for Sade's Sake*, Chan creates a moving tableau of sexual experimentation, shadow-puppet bodies engaging with one another in escalating erotic intensity. As the film continues, these 'shadow selves' begin to act as avatars, performing disturbing and violent sexual acts originally imagined in the novels of de Sade himself. Women are led on chains like dogs; heads are decapitated; bodies, once independent, become piles of monstrous orgiastic movement. The taboo nature of S&M is also reflected in Chan's use of shadow as his medium, making the spectral, unconscious parts of ourselves literal. If all this sounds a bit intense for a Sunday afternoon gallery stroll, you might be correct. And yet, with the shadow forms openly expressing what we ourselves should not, something quite beautiful emerges from Chan's work.

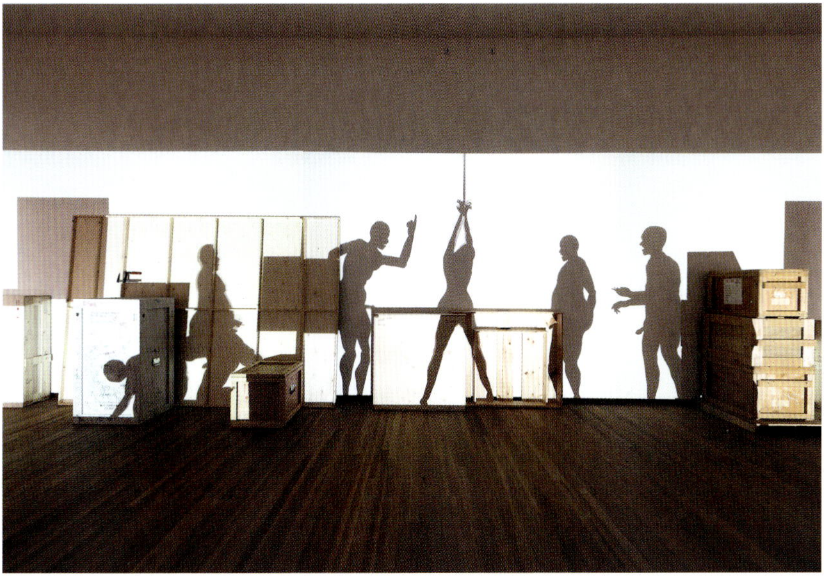

Paul Chan, *Sade for Sade's Sake*, 2009, digital video projection, 5 hours 45 minutes looped

BETTY TOMPKINS

Fuck Painting #31, 2009

Are you ready for your close-up?

In the same year that humankind went to the moon and the Manson murders shocked America, artist Betty Tompkins was rifling through her then-husband's pornography collection. It was in these images, acquired abroad to bypass US censorship laws, that Tompkins found inspiration for her first body of work: *Fuck Paintings*. Created using hundreds of layers of spray paint built up over stills of couples engaged in sex, her many variations each capture a raw, intimate moment. What interested Tompkins most were the mechanics of sex, and how, without the trappings of idealisation, this essential act could be made into art. To achieve this, Tompkins shows sex ultra close-up, with bodies, identities and emotional context erased from the image. By focusing purely on genitalia – and here, the ins and outs of the arrangement, so to speak – gender roles are eradicated, and dynamics like submission or domination are removed. The work toys with ideas around obscenity but, while the transgressive element is clear, Tompkins's close-up invites the viewer to see the penetrative act as something almost sculptural, softening the image and elevating it into art.

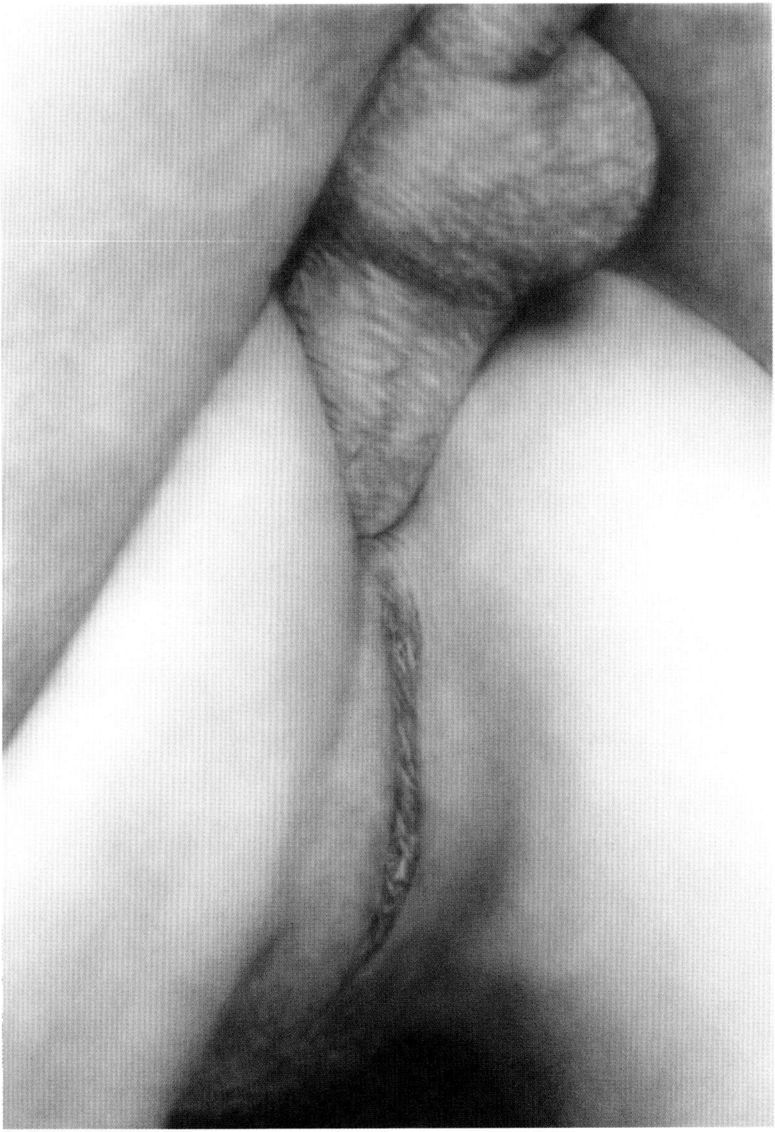

Betty Tompkins, *Fuck Painting #31*, 2009, acrylic on canvas, 203.2 × 162.6 cm

SUNIL GUPTA

Untitled #9 (from Sun City), 2010

Looking for sin in sun city

Responding to his own experiences as a gay man of Indian descent, Gupta created *Sun City*: a photographic series exploring sexuality, race and identity, and how to live an erotic life in the open – and in secret. Part of this includes Gupta's protagonist exploring the gay bathhouses that populate parts of Paris. In his series, Gupta borrowed from the highly stylised cinema of the 1960s, using depictions of the heterosexual hero driven by desire in films like *La Jetée* and translating them into a homosexual, immigrant context. In #9, Gupta's hero looks shyly around the room, surrounded by naked men adopting poses commonly seen in sculptures from antiquity. There is a sense of loneliness here; the bodies are on show, but everyone stands apart, making this erotic scene a manifestation of unreachable desire. Like a mirage, Gupta uses technicolour lighting to imbue the image with a painterly quality, his protagonist spotlit in yellow to suggest sanctity and innocence. As sensual as Gupta's vision is, *Sun City* is less about sin and more about a universal yearning for connection, and how we use bodies to find it.

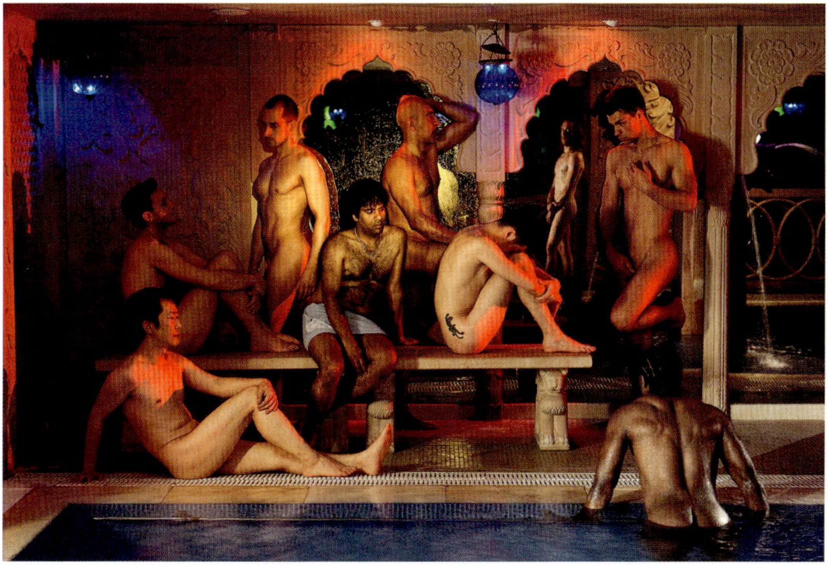

Sunil Gupta, *Untitled #9 (from Sun City)*, 2010

EKTOR GARCIA

manos a la obra, 2016

The glove that fits

ektor garcia (lowercase intended) is an artist who takes their craft seriously. Using his work to reflect on his queer experience, the Mexican-American artist deploys craft materials, both traditional and otherwise, to interrogate what we think of as erotic. Using leather, woven rubber and crochet, garcia explores his struggle to dominate his materials, mirroring the dynamics of submission and dominance in sexual relationships. In *manos a la obra*, which translates as 'let's do it' (wink), these materials are bent to garcia's will. A glove made from chainmail-like fabric is constructed using traditional crochet techniques, its prominence echoing the latex gloves associated with fetish wear. At the same time, the thick glove also alludes to Mexico's turbulent history as a nation colonised by Spanish conquistadors, who would have worn heavy metal gauntlets not unlike garcia's own creation. Through this multi-faceted symbolism, garcia's sculptural work merges the erotic with the geopolitical. Using materials like steel beaten into a rough cuboid, garcia imbues the work with a sensual charge, situating his own desires and experiences within the context of a wider ancestral history.

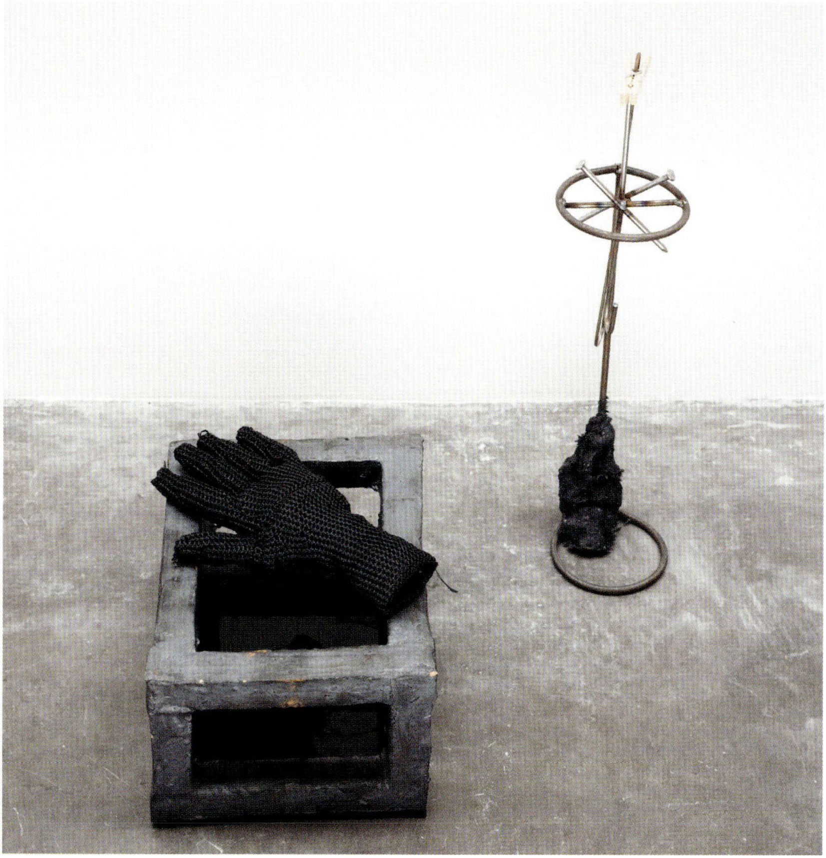

ektor garcia, *manos a la obra (let's do it)*, (detail), 2016, ceramic, glass, crochet, nuts, welded steel, welded nails, magnet, clothespin, 48.9 × 48.9 × 54 cm

KAT TORONTO/MISS MEATFACE

Miss Meatface Household Chores, 2017

Novel way to clean a bathroom

Following a battle with cervical cancer and a subsequent hysterectomy, the multidisciplinary artist Kat Toronto created her Miss Meatface alter-ego in 2014 as a way to interrogate and question what it means to be a woman. Often latex-bound and dressed in brightly coloured wigs, pearls and 1950s-style outfits, Miss Meatface combined the aesthetics of a glamorous tradwife with the club kid kink scene to create a fantasy of womanhood. In *Miss Meatface Household Chores*, we see her on all fours in a kitsch buttercup-yellow bathroom, a toilet brush gripped in her mouth. As everyday viewing, the image is pretty transgressive. Playing on themes of submissive femininity, the image of a doting housewife (a male fantasy for a male gaze) is parodied, while the fetishistic nature of this role is made literal, her pose making the degradation explicit and unabashed. Yet in her thigh-high boots and glistening black latex, Miss Meatface is the one in control – this self-portrait is a well-executed display of the push-and-pull between submission and domination. Unsubtle though it may be, it's a testament to how humour can challenge pre-conceived notions of gender and sexuality.

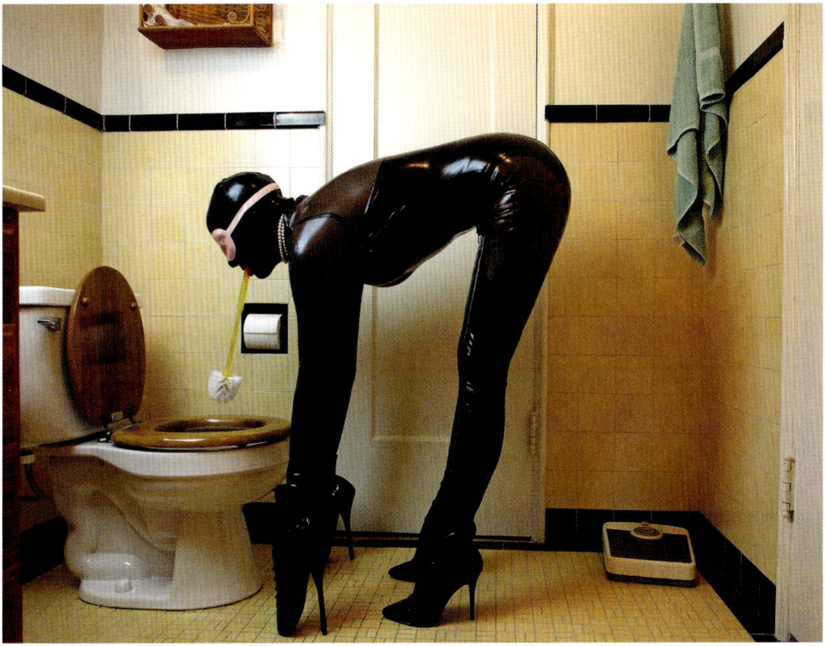

Kat Toronto/Miss Meatface, *Miss Meatface Household Chores*, 2017, digital photograph

SHANNON CARTIER LUCY

Morning Prayers, 2018

An ungodly situation

Shannon Cartier Lucy had an unconventional upbringing. Growing up with a parent who had schizophrenia, Lucy would come home to find toasters in the freezer, or a Bible in the dishwasher. These occurrences shaped her visual language, her artwork acting as snapshots of objects and people in situations they are not meant to be. In *Morning Prayers*, an uncanny visual is coupled with a frisson of sexual tension; a female figure kneels from the bed, her hands clasped in prayer on the floor and her trousers pulled down. At once jarring and visually arresting, the ordinary domestic space and dishevelled bedroom is cut through by the suggestiveness of her pose. Her devout, submissive stance raises more questions than answers. Is this an unorthodox Our Father? Or does the severity of the pose and her state of undress point to something more sinister, even violent? The artist seems less focused on creating a single narrative, instead looking to provoke a strong emotional response, recalling our past, or repressed, unconscious memory. Freud argues that erotic associations formed in childhood are accessed, as adults, through repressed or unconscious memory, and Lucy's work pulls from hazy childhood imagery to summon a simmering, pent-up erotic energy.

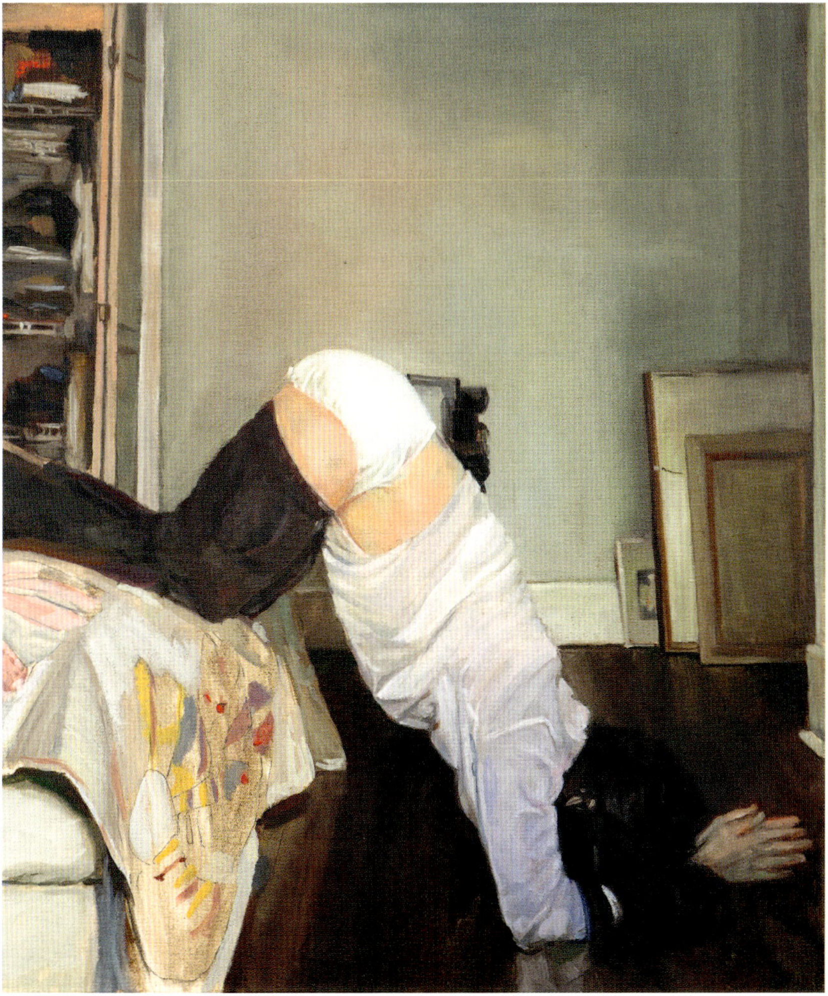

Shannon Cartier Lucy, *Morning Prayers*, 2018, oil on canvas, 55.9 × 48.3 cm

OH DE LAVAL

The Lover, 2019

Three's a crowd

Born Olga Pothipirom, the artist known as Oh de Laval creates work that revels in sexual misadventure. Her characters engage in ludicrous, slapstick-adjacent sex acts that thrum with a sense of menace. Painted in broad, quick brushstrokes, there is a cartoonish quality that allows de Laval to create scenes far removed from our own lived reality, allowing us to indulge in our most outrageous fantasies. In *The Lover*, a woman sits dressed in slipping, billowing lingerie as a buffoonish man aggressively grasps her breast. The scene is set in a lush and resplendent boudoir, evoking the kind of high camp interiors you'd expect from an imitation Louis XII chateaux. But a surprise lurks beneath the cushions: a naked figure hides within the sofa, his penis red and erect as the couple fumble above him. If this sounds like fine art *Carry On*-style, you wouldn't be wrong; de Laval conjures an entirely unconventional threesome. In this way, de Laval's work acts as a window into our most licentious desires, becoming a playground for erotic hedonism, where viewers can be voyeurs to acts of violence, perversion and spectacle.

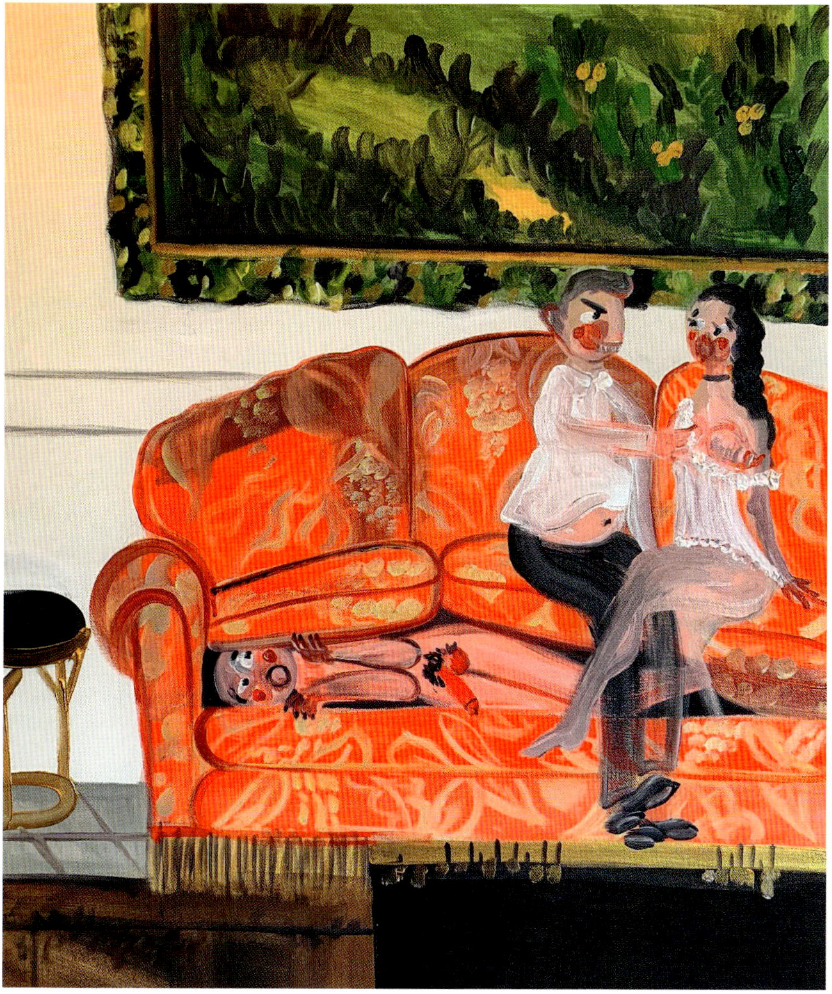

Oh de Laval, *The Lover*, 2019, acrylic on canvas, 60 × 76 cm

MARTHA SUMMERS

TOOLbelt, 2022

Erotic hardware

Can something that is useful also be erotic? This is one of the many themes at play in the work of architect, artist and designer Martha Summers, most notably in their seminal art piece *TOOLbelt*. Conceived in 2018 but materialised during the Covid-19 lockdown, *TOOLbelt* is a humorous yet earnest evocation of queer desire and erotic functionality. Designed to mimic the belts commonly used by tradespeople, Summers upends the heteronormative codes signified by the belt, turning it into a strap-on harness that can be used to sport dildos and other toys to facilitate sexual pleasure – certainly not your regular builders' garb. An autobiographical piece, Summers flexes the associated aesthetics of butch identity – one which does not seek to appease the male gaze and rejects the confines of sexualised, commodified femininity. Summers creates a work that is not only a useful tool for their community but also references their own experiences, reflecting the links between DIY and queerness, an existence often shaped by making, mending and crafting an identity. *TOOLbelt* operates on many levels – a finger-up to expectations, and an erotic work that offers much more than just a good time.

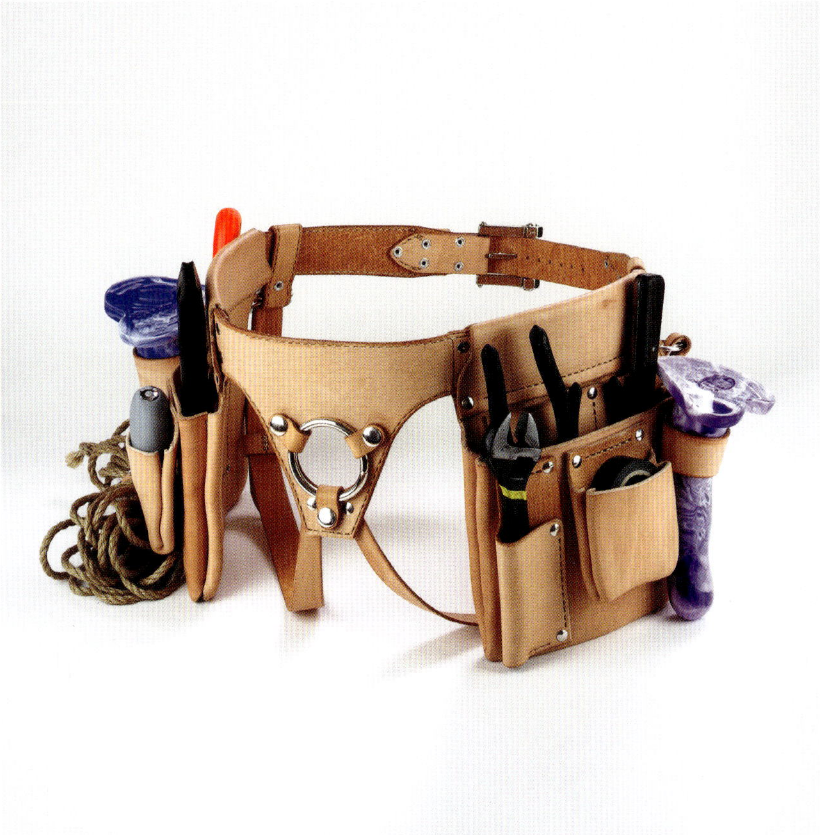

Martha Summers, *TOOLbelt*, 2022, vegan tan leather harness

LUCA GIOVAGNOLI

The Prayer, 2023

Upon close inspection

Luca Giovagnoli was raised in Rimini, where one of Italy's greatest auteurs, Federico Fellini, filmed many of his masterpieces. Giovagnoli's artistic sensibilities were shaped by the melodrama and high eroticism of these films and, seen, his paintings act like cinematic snapshots, or uneasy memories removed from their everyday context. In *The Prayer*, a man kneels before a woman who stands in heels, her back to the viewer. Her skirt is hitched high, and the man before her is worshipful. Bold brushstrokes create barely defined, anonymous faces – shifting, shapeless figures that exaggerate the already dreamlike scene. Key to Giovagnoli's work is the ambiguous portrayal of power relations. Is the man venerating himself at her feet? Or is she showcasing herself for approval, his eyes averted from her gaze not in reverence, but inspection? This enigma only heightens our curiosity. Viewers are drawn in, provided with a quasi-cinematic set piece on which to project uncomfortable desires.

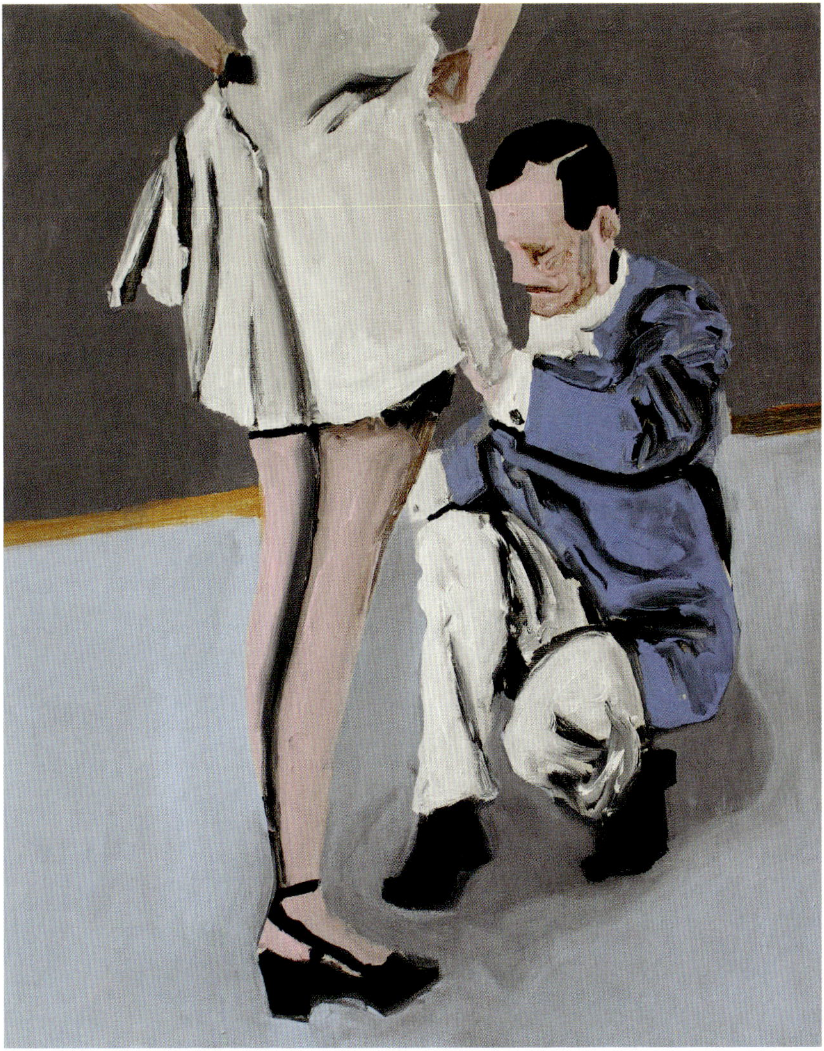

Luca Giovagnoli, *The Prayer*, 2023, acrylic on canvas, 60 × 50 cm

Further Reading

Love and the Erotic in Art by Stefano Zuffi
A richly illustrated exploration of how love, desire and the erotic have been depicted in art throughout history.

120 Days of Sodom by the Marquis de Sade
A notorious and controversial text depicting extreme sexual acts, it remains a foundational work in discussions of erotic literature.

The Art of Feminism edited by Helena Reckitt
A comprehensive guide to feminist art practices and their influence, featuring key artists and critical essays.

Hold it Against Me by Jennifer Doyle
An exploration of emotion and difficulty in contemporary art, examining how discomfort can provoke deeper engagement with artworks.

Vision and Difference by Griselda Pollock
A feminist analysis of how gender shapes the perception and production of visual art, challenging traditional art history and emphasising the need for a gender-aware critique of art institutions and representation.

The Erotic Arts by Peter Webb
A survey of eroticism in art, exploring its diverse forms and cultural significance across various historical periods.

Art and Pornography edited by Hans Maes and Jerrold Levinson
Philosophical essays discussing the intersection of art and pornography, questioning where art ends and exploitation begins.

Writing in Space by Lorraine O'Grady
A collection of essays blending autobiography and art criticism, reflecting on race, feminism and the art world.

Institutional Time by Judy Chicago
A critique of conventional studio art education, calling for more dynamic and experimental approaches to artistic learning. Chicago reflects on her personal experiences as an artist, pushing for innovation over tradition in art pedagogy.

Sex Objects by Jennifer Doyle
A critical examination of how desire and power dynamics are portrayed in art, with a focus on feminist theory.

A Critical Dictionary of Pyschoanalysis by Charles Rycroft
A comprehensive reference to Freud's psychoanalytic concepts, essential for understanding his theories on sexuality and the unconscious.

Masochism: Coldness and Cruelty & Venus in Furs by Giles Deleuze
Deleuze's philosophical exploration of masochism, paired with the classic novella that inspired his study.

Artist Directory

Marina Abramović

b.1946, Belgrade, Serbia

A pioneer in performance art, Abramović is known for her endurance-based works that explore physical and mental limits, examining themes of time, pain and human connection.

Ron Athey

b.1961, Connecticut, USA

An American performance artist, Athey is known for his intense and extreme performances that focus on body modification, desire, sexuality, religion and trauma.

Francis Bacon

b.1909, Dublin, Ireland
d.1992, Madrid, Spain

An Irish-born British figurative painter, Bacon is celebrated for his abstracted and unsettling figures, often presented as sequences or triptychs. Fascinated by the brutality of modern life, his work delves into the darker aspects of the human psyche, illuminating our inner psychological turmoil.

Aubrey Beardsley

b.1872, Brighton, UK
d.1898, Menton, France

An English illustrator and author, Beardsley is known for his highly stylised and often erotic illustrations that defied the repressive social mores of Victorian England. His art, glamorous and subversive, left a lasting impact on the Aesthetic movement.

Lynda Benglis

b.1941, Louisiana, USA

An American sculptor and visual artist, Benglis is famed for her wax paintings, controversial self-portraits and multimedia work. Her provocative *Artforum Advertisement* remains a seminal moment in feminist art history.

Gian Lorenzo Bernini

b.1598, Naples, Italy
d.1680, Rome, Italy

An Italian sculptor and architect, Bernini is credited with developing the Baroque style of sculpture. His theatrical, dynamic works aimed to evoke strong emotional responses in viewers, capturing intense moments of human expression and divine interaction.

Hans Bellmer

b.1902, Kattowitz (now Katowice), Poland
d.1975, Paris, France

A German artist best known for his surreal, life-sized female dolls, Bellmer's work fuses eroticism and body horror. His drawings, sculptures and etchings are closely associated with the Surrealist movement, reflecting the trauma of living through both World Wars.

Auguste Belloc

b.1800, Montrabé, France
d.1867, Paris, France

A French artist who began as a painter and watercolourist before transitioning to photography, Belloc is best known for his erotic and nude photographic works, which were considered groundbreaking in their time.

Paul Chan

b.1973, Hong Kong, China

An American multimedia artist, Chan draws inspiration from outsider artists, philosophers and playwrights such as Henry Darger, Samuel Beckett and the Marquis de Sade. His work, which includes single-channel videos, projections and animations, often explores themes of sex, violence and globalisation.

Judy Chicago

b.1939, Chicago, USA

Born Judith Sylvia Cohen, Chicago is an American feminist artist, educator and academic. She is best known for her large-scale installations, paintings and drawings, which focus on female experiences, sexuality and self-expression.

Ithell Colquhoun

b.1906, Shillong, India
d.1988, Cornwall, UK

A British artist and occultist, Colquhoun is most noted for her associations with Surrealism. Her paintings combine the ethereal beauty of the natural world with surreal, often erotic scenes.

Gustave Courbet

b.1819, Ornans, France
d.1877, La Tour-de-Peilz, Switzerland

A leading figure of the Realism movement in mid-19th-century France, Courbet rejected Romanticism and idealism, instead portraying everyday scenes with a bold social critique.

Salvador Dalí

b.1904, Figueres, Spain
d.1989, Figueres, Spain

A Spanish artist and a key figure in Surrealism, Dalí is famous for his bizarre, dreamlike paintings filled with symbolic imagery that explores themes like death, desire and memory.

Achille Devéria

b.1800, Paris, France
d.1857, Paris, France

A French painter and lithographer, Devéria was known for his portraits of famous writers and artists but gained particular fame for his erotic artworks and libertine engravings.

Jean Dubuffet

b.1901, Le Havre, France
d.1985, Paris, France

A renegade French painter and sculptor, Dubuffet founded the Art Brut movement, advocating for art created outside traditional aesthetic standards. He was inspired by 'outsider' and non-Western art, rejecting conventional ideas of beauty, and became particularly influential in the United States.

Marcel Duchamp

b.1887, Blainville-Crevon, France
d.1968, Neuilly-sur-Seine, France

Often hailed as the father of Conceptual Art, Duchamp was a painter, sculptor and chess player whose work straddled Cubism and Dada. He revolutionised art by assigning new meaning to everyday objects.

Marlene Dumas
b.1953, Cape Town, South Africa
A South African artist now based in the Netherlands, Dumas creates powerful portraits that explore female sexuality, desire and the darker aspects of human existence. Working in paint, collage and ink, her art often addresses complex themes like race, guilt, violence and tenderness.

Tracey Emin
b.1963, London, UK
A key figure in the Young British Artists (YBAs), Emin is known for her provocative works in paint, mixed media and photography. Her art often focuses on her personal experiences, particularly those related to sex and trauma, conveyed with striking candour and emotional intensity.

Jacob Epstein
b.1880, NYC, USA
d.1959, London, UK
An American-British sculptor, Epstein was a Modernist pioneer known for his emphasis on simplicity and form over the ornate classical style. His bold, often controversial works explored sexuality and the human body.

Leonor Fini
b.1907, Buenos Aires, Argentina
d.1996, Paris, France
An Argentine-born artist who grew up in Italy, Fini was a Surrealist painter, designer and illustrator. Her work features depictions of powerful women, often with erotic undertones, challenging traditional gender roles and embracing themes of female empowerment.

Jean-Honoré Fragonard
b.1732, Grasse, France
d.1806, Paris, France
A painter and printmaker of the Rococo era, Fragonard was beloved by the French nobility for his light, intimate scenes. His works, often featuring playful, romantic and erotic themes, are emblematic of the frivolity and sensuality of the period.

ektor garcia
b.1985, California, USA
A Mexican-American multidisciplinary artist, garcia works with traditional craft techniques such as crochet and weaving, using found materials to explore themes of identity, belonging and sexuality.

Luca Giovagnoli
b.1963, Rimini, Italy
An Italian painter, Giovagnoli is known for his bold figurative works that explore themes of eroticism. Influenced by the golden age of Italian cinema, his paintings often evoke cinematic scenes, blending sensuality and mystery.

Sarah Goodridge
b.1788, Massachusetts, USA
d.1853, Boston, USA
An American artist, Goodridge specialised in portrait miniatures. While she painted many prominent politicians and fellow artists of her time, she is most remembered for

her intimate self-portrait, *Beauty Revealed*, depicting her bare breasts.

Duncan Grant
b.1885, Rothiemurchus, Scotland
d.1978, Aldermaston, Scotland
A Scottish painter, designer and textile artist, Grant was a central figure in the Bloomsbury Group. His avant-garde, Modernist work ranged from portraits to decorative arts. After his death, a collection of erotic drawings, many celebrating queer love, was discovered, adding depth to his legacy.

Sunil Gupta
b.1953, New Delhi, India
An Indian-born Canadian photographer, Gupta's work explores his experience as a gay man of Indian descent. His photographs address themes of sexual identity, migration, race and the meaning of family.

Barbara Hepworth
b.1903, Yorkshire, UK
d.1975, St Ives, UK
A British Modernist artist, Hepworth was inspired by the undulating landscapes of her Yorkshire upbringing. Known for her organic, sensuous forms in sculpture, drawing and painting, she played a central role in the St Ives Group and was a founder of the Unit One art movement, influencing mid-20th-century Abstraction.

Hokusai
b.1760, Edo (now Tokyo), Japan
d.1849, Edo, Japan
A Japanese painter and printmaker of the Edo period (1603–1868), Hokusai is best known for his iconic woodblock landscapes. His work, which also includes erotic prints known as Shunga, had a profound influence on Western artists like Vincent Van Gogh and Claude Monet.

Allen Jones
b.1937, Southampton, UK
A British Pop artist, Jones gained fame and notoriety for his provocative sculptures featuring highly sexualised female mannequins posed as inanimate furniture.

Georgia O'Keeffe
b.1887, Wisconsin, USA
d.1986, Santa Fe, USA
Known as the 'Mother of American Modernism', O'Keeffe is celebrated for her abstract, sensual depictions of flowers, which are often interpreted as symbolic of female genitalia. Her work, spanning over six decades, includes landscapes and cityscapes that contributed to her iconic status.

Gustav Klimt
b.1862, Baumgarten, Austria
d.1918, Vienna, Austria
An Austrian Symbolist painter and a founding member of the Viennese Secession, Klimt is best known for his portraits of women and his richly decorative style, as well as his erotic drawings of the female form.

Oh de Laval
b.1990, Bangkok, Thailand
Born Olga Pothipirom, de Laval is a Polish-Thai painter who creates

fantastical, provocative figurative erotic works. Infusing humour and elements of popular culture, her surreal paintings explore how pleasure and fantasy interact.

Lee Lozano
b.1930, Newark, USA
d.1999, Dallas, USA
Lee Lozano moved to New York in the 1960s and became a prominent figure in the art scene, renowned for her enigmatic sexualised paintings of utility objects as well as her conceptual work. Known for her radical *Dropout Piece*, she left the art world at the age of 40, rejecting its commercial and social systems.

Sarah Lucas
b.1962, London, UK
A British artist associated with the Young British Artists movement, Lucas is known for her provocative sculptures, photographs and collages laced with humour and satire that explore sexuality and gender.

Shannon Cartier Lucy
b.1977, Nashville, USA
An American figurative painter, Lucy's surreal oil paintings often depict domestic spaces infused with an uncanny, erotic tension. Her works blend the ordinary with the hyperreal, creating unsettling narratives that blur the lines between reality and fantasy.

René Magritte
b.1898, Lessines, Belgium
d.1967, Brussels, Belgium
A key figure in the Surrealist movement, Magritte is known for his thought-provoking depictions of familiar objects in strange contexts, blurring the boundaries between dream and reality.

Édouard Manet
b.1832, Paris, France
d.1883, Paris, France
A pioneering French Modernist painter, Manet's work marked a shift from Realism to Impressionism, capturing scenes of contemporary French life with bold brushstrokes. His groundbreaking pieces, helped redefine modern art, making him one of France's most famous artists.

Michealangelo
b.1475, Caprese, Italy
d.1564, Rome, Italy
One of the most renowned artists of the Italian Renaissance, Michelangelo was a master sculptor, painter and architect. His works have become enduring symbols of Renaissance artistry and humanistic ideals.

Daidō Moriyama
b.1938, Osaka, Japan
A revolutionary Japanese photographer, Moriyama is best known for his raw, grainy black-and-white street photography that captures the chaotic energy of urban life.

Jean le Noir
active c.1335–1380, France
A celebrated manuscript illuminator, Jean le Noir worked in France during the 14th century, where he created richly detailed works for religious

manuscripts. His most famous illumination is the *Psalter of Bonne de Luxembourg*, known for its intricate and expressive detail.

Catherine Opie
b.1961, Ohio, USA
An American fine art photographer, Opie's work explores themes of identity, focusing on the intimate lives of the LGBTQ+ community and other marginalised groups in the USA.

Raphaelle Peale
b.1774, Maryland, USA
d.1825, Philadelphia, USA
An American still-life painter, Peale's meticulously detailed still-life compositions often featured fruit and natural produce, reflect a quiet, contemplative approach to painting.

Man Ray
b.1890, Philadelphia, USA
d.1976, Paris, France
Born Emmanuel Radnitzky, Man Ray was an American visual artist who made significant contributions to both the Dada and Surrealist movements. He was renowned for his avant-garde photography, fashion photography and experimental art.

Francesco Salviati
b.1510, Florence, Italy
d.1563, Rome, Italy
An Italian painter of the late Renaissance, Salviati worked in the Mannerist style, characterised by exaggerated proportions and idealised beauty.

Joan Semmel
b.1932, New York, USA
An American painter, Semmel is known for her bold, large-scale erotic works that often depict her own nude body or couples engaged in sexual intimacy. Her use of vibrant, unnatural colours and the centring of the female gaze challenge traditional depictions of the female form and sexuality.

Carolee Schneemann
b.1939, Pennsylvania, USA
d.2019, New York, USA
An American visual artist, Schneemann is celebrated for her radical multimedia work, blending dance, performance, film and painting to interrogate the body, sexuality and gender.

Egon Schiele
b.1890, Tulln, Austria
d.1918, Vienna Austria
An Austrian Expressionist painter, Schiele is renowned for his raw, unidealised depictions of the human body, particularly his nudes. His intimate works reveal the emotional and psychological complexities of his sitters, often reflecting turbulent relationships.

Walter Sickert
b.1860, Munich, Germany
d.1942, Bath, UK
A German-born British painter and printmaker, Sickert's work marked a transition period from Impressionism to Modernism, with a focus on depicting ordinary people and urban scenes.

Martha Summers
b.1980, London, UK
An architect, artist and designer, Summers' work is informed by their architectural training and explores themes of queer domesticity, self-fashioning and butch identity.

Wolfgang Tillmans
b.1968, Remscheid, Germany
Tillmans is known for his diverse body of work that captures the nuances of everyday life. His observational photography covers a broad spectrum, from still lifes and portraits to abstract works, exploring themes of identity, community and the passage of time.

Titian
b.1488, Pieve di Cadore, Italy
d.1576, Venice, Italy
A Renaissance Master, Titian was one of the most influential Italian painters of his time, sought after by European nobility for his portraits, religious scenes and mythological compositions.

Tom of Finland
b.1920, Kaarina, Finland
d.1991, Helsinki, Finland
Born Touko Valio Laaksonen, Tom of Finland became famous for his homoerotic illustrations, depicting hyper-masculine men in sexually charged homoerotic scenes. His work had a profound influence on late 20th-century gay culture, pushing the boundaries of erotic art and LGBTQ+ representation.

Kat Toronto
b.1980, California, USA
Known as 'Miss Meatface', Toronto is an American multidisciplinary artist whose work spans performance and photography to explore themes of femininity, gender, submission and domination.

Betty Tompkins
b.1945, Washington D.C., USA
An American artist, Tompkins is a pioneer of feminist art, known for her series 'Fuck Paintings', which features photorealistic depictions of close-up sexual acts.

Henri de Toulouse-Lautrec
b.1864, Albi, France
d.1901, Saint-André-du-Bois, France
A French painter, caricaturist and printmaker, Toulouse-Lautrec chronicled the vibrant life of late 19th-century Paris, chronicling the decadent lives of the upper and working classes.

Francisco de Zurbarán
b.1598, Fuente de Cantos, Spain
d.1664, Madrid, Spain
A Spanish Baroque painter, Zurbarán is known for his masterful use of chiaroscuro and his deeply religious works, often depicting monks, nuns and martyrs.

Picture credits

The Venus of Willendorf, 30000–25000 BCE (limestone coloured with red ochre) © Ali Meyer / Bridgeman Images; Oinochoe © Heritage Image Partnership Ltd / Alamy Stock Photo; India / Bangladesh: A lovemaking scene, Sunga Dynasty © Pictures from History / Bridgeman Images; Pompeii © Public Domain; Ornate statues on two or three tiers on Vishwanath temple © Dinodia / Bridgeman Images; Kilpeck Sheela-na-gig © Steve Taylor ARPS / Alamy Stock Photo; Christ's Side Wound © Public Domain; Leda and the Swan © The National Gallery, London; Venus, known as the Venus of Urbino © Titian / Photo © Stefano Baldini / Bridgeman Images; Agnus Dei © Francisco de Zurbarán. Bridgeman Images; Ecstasy of St. Teresa © Bernini. Alinari / Bridgeman Images; Triumph of the Phallus © The Trustees of the British Museum; The Swing © Jean-Honoré Fragonard. Wallace Collection, London, UK / Bridgeman Images; The Dream of the Fisherman's Wife © Hokusai. Pictures from History / Bridgeman Images; Still Life–A Deception–Venus Rising from a Bath © Alamy Stock Photo; Beauty Revealed © Public Domain; Olympia © Édouard Manet. Bridgeman Images; Artist and Sitter: manual foreplay © The Stapleton Collection / Bridgeman Images; Untitled, Auguste Belloc © Antiq-Photo Gallery, Paris; The Origin of the World © Gustave Courbet. Bridgeman Images; In bed: The kiss © Henri de Toulouse-Lautrec. Christie's Images / Bridgeman Images; The Lacedaemonian Ambassadors © Public Domain; The Wrestlers © Estate of Duncan Grant. All rights reserved. DACS 2024. Image © The Bloomsbury Workshop, London / Bridgeman Images; La Hollandaise artwork © Walter Sickert, image © Tate; Woman in Black Stockings © Artefact / Alamy Stock Photo; Reclining Nude with Drapery © Public Domain; Doves artwork © Jacob Epstein, image © Tate; The Kiss © Man Ray 2015 Trust / DACS, London 2024; Black Iris © Georgia O'Keeffe. The Metropolitan Museum of Art/ Art Resource/Scala, Florence; The Great Masturbator © Salvador Dalí, Fundació Gala-Salvador Dalí, DACS 2024, image © Index Fototeca / Bridgeman Images; The Doll © Hans Bellmer. ADAGP, Paris and DACS, London 2024; Scylla artwork © Ithell Colquhoun, image © Tate; The Shepherdess of the Sphinxes © Leonor Fini. Peggy Guggenheim Collection, Venice (Solomon R. Guggenheim Foundation, New York). Image © ADAGP, Paris and DACS, London 2024; Wave artwork © Barbara Hepworth, courtesy Barbara Hepworth Estate, image © National Galleries Scotland, artwork purchased with support from The National Lottery Heritage

An Opinionated Guide to Erotic Art
First edition

Published in 2024 by Hoxton Mini Press, London

Text by Elise Bell
Editing by Zoë Jellicoe
Production design by Dom Grant
Series design by Tom Etherington
Proofreading by Florence Ward

Thank you to all of the individuals and institutions who have provided images and arranged permissions. While every effort has been made to trace the present copyright holders we apologise in advance for any unintentional omission or error, and would be pleased to insert the appropriate acknowledgement in any subsequent edition.

A CIP catalogue record for this book is available from the British Library.

ISBN: 978-1-914314-71-1

Printed and bound by Finidr, Czechia

Hoxton Mini Press is an environmentally conscious publisher, committed to offsetting our carbon footprint. This book is 100 per cent carbon compensated, with offset purchased from Stand For Trees.

Every time you order from our website, we plant a tree:
www.hoxtonminipress.com

FSC
www.fsc.org
MIX
Paper from
responsible sources
FSC® C014138